A Bergsonian Bridge to Phenomenological Psychology

Current Continental Research is co-published by The Center for Advanced Research in Phenomenology and University Press of America, Inc.

CURRENT CONTINENTAL RESEARCH 204

Helmut R. Wagner

with Ilja Srubar

A BERGSONIAN BRIDGE TO PHENOMENOLOGICAL PSYCHOLOGY

1984

Center for Advanced Research in Phenomenology
& University Press of America, Washington, D.C.

University Press of America,™ Inc.

4720 Boston Way
Lanham, MD 20706

3 Henrietta Street
London WC2E 8LU England

Printed in the United States of America

ISBN (Perfect): 0-8191-4395-2
ISBN (Cloth): 0-8191-4394-4

All University Press of America books are produced on acid-free paper which exceeds the minimum standards set by the National Historical Publications and Records Commission.

ACKNOWLEDGEMENTS

The author is most obliged to Lester Embree. In 1975, he read my first account of Schutz's encounter with Bergson, written in preparation of the Schutz biography. His comments made it necessary for me to re-think my original evaluation of Schutz's first and unfinished project and to recognize its rather direct relevance for his later work. Eight years later, he welcomed my suggestion to submit the present study to The Center for Advanced Research in Phenomenology for inclusion in the series, CURRENT CONTINENTAL RESEARCH, and took the necessary steps for its acceptance.

An intermediate version of the manuscript was submitted to a referee for CCR. I am greatly obliged to him for his many comments, queries, and suggestions; they helped me considerably in bringing this study into its final shape. The responsibility for possible flaws in it, of course, remains my own.

The publishers of the English translation of Alfred Schutz's LIFE FORMS AND MEANING STRUCTURE, Routledge and Kegan Paul (London), have granted permission to include longer verbatim passages from this work into the present study. I acknowledge this with thanks.

Last but not least, the preparation and publication of this study was made possible by the continuing support of my research activities by the administration of Hobart and William Smith Colleges.

CONTENTS

INTRODUCTION

This monograph deals with an early phase in the life work of Alfred Schutz. This should have been stated in a subtitle which, however, had to be omitted for technical reasons. As author, I realize that this omission gives the main title a general ring which may evoke expectations which this study does not fulfill. I can only hope that, after this warning, readers will be prepared to accept its limited scope. The bridge to which the title referred was designed by Schutz who, however, stopped its construction well before its completion. In this introduction, I shall try to explain why this unfinished project deserves the attention it has received in this study.

TOPIC AND FOCUS

The writings of Alfred Schutz have become part of the literature of the international phenomenological movement. His contributions to it were co-determined by the fact that he came to phenomenology not from philosophy but from the social sciences; they gained their characteristic features from his general objective: to give the social sciences, and in particular sociology, a psychological-phenomenological basis.

Schutz was born in Vienna in 1899, and died in New York in 1959. In 1939, he came to the United States, having published his fundamental study, DER SINNHAFTE AUFBAU DER SOZIALEN WELT (1932), and having subsequently become a close friend and informal student of Edmund Husserl. Together with Herbert Spiegelberg and a few other refugee philosophers, he associated himself with Marvin Farber, one of the few American students of Husserl, who started the journal PHILOSOPHY AND PHENOMENOLOGICAL RESEARCH (PPR) and with it got the American phenomenological movement going. Both in Europe and the United States, Schutz made his living in business positions; he was a spare-time scholar. Yet, he managed to publish about twenty-five articles and essays during his American years, scattered over about a dozen journals and symposia volumes. He died, virtually unknown beyond the small circles of his students and of phenomenologists residing in the United States [1].

Today, practically all of his publications and a large part of his unpublished manuscripts are accessible in English and German editions, and some of them have been translated into one or several of five other languages. The present study has been occasioned by the recent publication of the manuscripts of an investigation Schutz undertook during 1924-1928 but left unfinished. The German edition is called

THEORIE DER LEBENSFORMEN (1981); the English LIFE FORMS AND MEANING STRUCTURE (1982).

This investigation is not only of biographical interest as Schutz's first serious scholarly undertaking, started at least six years before he began DER SINNHAFTE AUFBAU. It is of scholarly interest because it was his first attempt at radicalizing Max Weber's sociology of action and understanding by giving the 'subjective' concepts of meaning, motivation, and understanding an adequate 'psychological' foundation - the term 'phenomenological' not yet part of his vocabulary. This, however, was also the first and main objective of his book of 1932. The difference was that, in the earlier project, he tried to build a bridge between Weber's sociology and Henri Bergson's intuitionist philosophy; in the second project, Husserl largely but by far not completely replaced Bergson.

Schutz had planned to write his study in three parts. The first was to comprise what he called a "Theory of Life Forms," actually a pheno-psychological theory of consciousness as baseline for the development of a consistently subjective theory of forms and conditions of social experience. The latter was to be developed in the central second part, labelled "The Structure of the Objectivation of Meaning." The last part, finally, was to be devoted to "Object and Method of the Social Sciences." When Schutz abandoned this project, he had on hand the extensive yet unfinished first part. Further, he had three drafts of essays which, in form independent, were crucial contributions to the second part: analyses of the "Meaning structures" of language, of the literary art forms, and of music. They too were incomplete.

The German - documentary - edition of the LIFE FORMS was competently prepared by Ilja Srubar of the Sozialwissenschaftliche Archiv at Constance University. He had the opportunity to offer a much needed detailed introduction to the book, amounting to about one quarter of its pages. By contrast, it was decided - for reasons of space economy - to omit a comparative introduction to the British edition. Since I am responsible for the latter, this omission weighted heavily on my scholarly conscience. Finally, I decided to rework my original part of the introduction - Srubar had been assigned the other one - and to expand it into a study of its own: the present book.

This decision brought me face to face with the question: What purpose(s) should this undertaking serve? And this question, again, cannot be separated from the second one: And what audience(s) should it address? As long as I thought in terms of an introduction to the volume on LIFE FORMS, the answer to the second question was easy: the readers of the volume; and this facilitated the determination of its purposes. In general terms, these were intrinsic to content and objectives of Schutz's early project. In the first line, it was desirable to provide keys for a better understanding of the Bergson manuscripts:

first drafts lacking the careful editing Schutz devoted to his publications, made more difficult on account of their being forays into scholarly territories heretofore unknown to him. Secondly, those who were reaching for this posthumous volume would do so because they were familiar with at least parts of his later work and were interested in it. Having them in mind, I set down the central purpose of the present study: offering a critical-interpretative appraisal of Schutz's earliest project, outline its contribution to the development of his thinking in terms of his emerging intellectual "plan for life," and consequently determine its place in the body of his work as a whole [2].

When speaking of an audience reasonably familiar with Schutz's work and having an interest in it, I excluded readers who would set out to find access to his work; there is other literature to serve this purpose. On the other hand, I had not solely in mind readers who have largely or wholly accepted a Schutzian approach in their own teaching and research activities but also such who present largely different approaches within the large spectrum of the phenomenological movement as a whole - or, rather, those among them who wish to keep abreast of developments in other areas. Finally, in the case of Schutz it is important to keep in mind that a good if not the larger part of an audience who is receptive to his work is not affiliated with academic philosophy but with social-scientific disciplines. I hold it rather unlikely that the "interest in Schutz" by the one group is identical with that of the other.

This alone makes for two potential audiences rather than one. If this causes some inconsistencies in the direction in which I am beaming my representations, so be it. Under these circumstances, no author can do more than try. In the end, the effectiveness of his expositions and suggestions does not depend on imagined readers, but on his actual readers, that is, how they receive what he intends to offer. And, hopefully, they will exceed that intelligence which an author ascribes to his ad hoc construction of the ideal(-typical) reader.

Nevertheless, I hope that, in some way or other, I have managed to pursue the last and most important purpose of this study in a manner which appeals to both circles of my potential readers. I am referring to the crucial characteristics of Schutz's developing the arguments embodied in the Bergson study: frequently, he developed them beyond the target points set by Bergsonian presuppositions, transcending a given framework and prolonging the resulting baseline into unanticipated directions. I considered it my task to mark out these points of transcendence, ascertain the direction in which Schutz moved, fix the points at which he stopped, and project the lines further. They all, I found, pointed toward positions which, a few years later, he should clearly describe in his second project, that of DER SINNHAFTE AUFBAU.

Maybe, some phenomenologists will find such intellectual biographical items of no interest: Why speak of the paths and maybe detours by which a thinker arrived at his basic positions, when the latter are fully available? There is not much I can say in response. It is anyone's privilege to approach a "text" hermeneutically and, to say the least, relegate the author into the background. For me, the attempt at ascertaining the intentions of a scholar remains significant; I believe that a recognition of the ways in which he reached his basic conclusions goes a long way toward clarification of these intentions and make me to understand better not only them but also the theoretic-philosophical meanings of his finished thoughts.

In the present case, the recognition of Schutz's early efforts to achieve by way of Bergson alone what he later accomplished by marshalling Husserl's help, sheds a different light on the fact that Bergson never ceased to play an important role in his ongoing work. In addition, it may help to upgrade the recognition of Bergson as a writer who, in his earlier phenomenal-psychological investigations, had lasting contributions to make - contributions which are not annulled by his later philosophical flights into an universal evolutionism of his own making.

PREPARATION

My occupation with Schutz's manuscripts of the Bergson period goes back to 1974, when Mrs. Schutz gave me full access to the literary estate of her husband. I was then at the start of my work on the intellectual biography of Schutz. For this purpose, I made raw translations of Schutz's Bergson manuscripts and, in 1975, wrote two chapters dealing with them [3].

Before the literary estate of Schutz was microfilmed and became available to archives in Germany and North America in 1977, the existence of a study by Schutz, which antedated his major publication DER SINNHAFTE AUFBAU DER SOZIALEN WELT (1932) and was based entirely on Bergson, was no more than a rumor even among Schutz's direct students. In 1977, Philosophy and Phenomenological Research published my appraisal of "The Bergsonian Period of Alfred Schutz," the first public account of the project on LIFE FORMS AND MEANING STRUCTURE [4]. Between Spring 1979 and early Winter 1980, I worked intermittently on bringing my translations of the various manuscripts into their final shape. This gave me the occasion to rescrutinize them and to collect a good amount of notes which I used, in conjunction with the Bergson chapters of the extended biography of Schutz, for the critical appraisal which makes up the bulk of the present book.

PART I

SCHUTZ'S BERGSONIAN PERIOD

This study is concerned with Schutz's explorations of areas of a psychology of consciousness which were brought together in his book, LIFE FORMS AND MEANING STRUCTURE. Its first part offers a sketch of the intellectual and philosophical circumstances under which Schutz decided to develop Max Weber's rudimentary sociology of understanding into a consistent and comprehensive theory, gives a survey of the ideas and conceptions which Bergson offered him for this purpose, outlines systematically the theory of life forms which resulted from his efforts, inspects the limits to which Schutz used Bergson's work, and conveys an idea of the transitional character of his Bergsonian period, which lasted from 1924 to 1928.

Each of the topics mentioned forms a chapter. The second and third ones have been contributed by Ilja Srubar, the editor of the German edition of LIFE FORMS AND MEANING STRUCTURE. In conjunction with the other three, they should serve the purposes laid out in the Introduction to this volume.

CHAPTER 1

THE MOVE TOWARD BERGSON

SOCIOLOGY OF UNDERSTANDING AND PSYCHOLOGY OF CONSCIOUSNESS

At the end of 1918, Alfred Schutz returned from the battle fields in Northern Italy, and subsequently studied Law and Economics at the university of his native Vienna. This study prepared him for a business career which should secure his livelihood for all but the last two-and-a-half years of his adult life. Yet, his true intellectual interests remained outside his vocational studies and commitments. His main teachers - notably Hans Kelsen (International Law) and Ludwig von Mises (Theory of Marginal Utility) fascinated him by the high level of their theoretical reasoning. In them, he encountered strands of the tradition of the German Geisteswissenschaften, a strictly humanist approach to social-science matters. He respected both although he developed considerable reservations with regard to their theories. He accepted Kelsen's theory of Positive Law insofar as it lent itself to sociological interpretations but found his purely normative theory of Society untenable. Likewise, he accepted Mises's theory of marginal utility insofar as it made human actors - in their roles as consumers - into crucial factors in socio-economic processes, but he rejected both his extreme laissez-faire position and his claim that economic laws are apriorily valid.

It was only after a hectic and condensed study period that Schutz defined his own place in the scholarly world: he decided to become a sociologist after the image he had made himself of Max Weber - probably more under the influence of his co-students than his teachers. His first post-doctoral project was the study of Weber's writings, mainly of his last work, WIRTSCHAFT UND GESELLSCHAFT, and of his collected methodological essays.

Schutz had no intention to become an exponent and interpreter of Weber's total work in its array of large-scale topical interests and its broad historical dimensions. Rather, he focused on a small section of it; the conceptual-methodological outline of what is now called Weber's interpretative sociology or his sociology of social action and understanding [1]. Its extremely condensed exposition fills hardly more than the first twenty pages of WIRTSCHAFT UND GESELLSCHAFT. Yet, it contains all the notions and conceptions which, in Schutz's opinion, made Weber into the great pioneer of a sociological approach which ascribed to the human individual, with his or her interests and volitions, the central place in all social-scientific concerns. Forthwith, Schutz's own scholarly efforts should be devoted to the clarification, development, and consistent application of these principles of Weber.

As social science, however, sociology of understanding was in need of a suitable theoretical method which, also, had been brought to the fore by Weber. He was not its inventor but he made it from an underlying procedure of social scientists of a geisteswissenschaftliche persuasion into a theoretically developed overt method: the method of ideal-typical analysis. Ideal types were empirically derived concepts which contain, e.g., only those features of social actors or their 'typical' conduct which gave the latter their theoretical significance in terms of a sociologist's theoretical frame of reference. They lead to pure types - ideal in this sense - without the interference of all the empirically ever present traits or tendencies which do not agree with the given theoretical principle. For instance, the ideal types of rational actors and of rational actions show both as they would occur if the actors would follow purely rational purposes and had the appropriate knowledge to carry them out without errors. In daily social life, this is a fictitious assumption. It is, however, highly useful in that it operates on a theoretically at least comparatively simple basis and allows to explain the empirical deviations from theoretical expectations in a sociologically satisfactory manner. It provides also for the investigation of disturbing factors and thus arrives at interpretations which do justice to the schemes of actual human conduct which are ever much more complex than any theoretical schemes. - In all of Schutz's work, the ideal-typical method, as viewed and interpreted by him, was the cornerstone of all sociological procedure, whether he was concerned with the construction of theoretical-conceptual frames or with empirical investigations.

Next to the quite substantial restrictions of Schutz's active interest in Weber's work, the concentration on the sociology of understanding and the ideal typical method, a second restriction of his acceptance of Weber must be mentioned: it was critical. He was immensely impressed by the genius of this scholarly giant; but he was not accepting him blindly. The outlines of the sociology of understanding were written down hastily by a thinker who had no patience with theoretical preliminaries, confined them to what he considered the bare essentials, so as to rush on to the substantive investigations which were his true concern. Schutz, of an intellectual temperament which was the opposite of that of Weber, could reconcile himself neither with the sketchiness of Weber's formulations nor with what he considered its flaws and equivocations: The introductory pages of WIRTSCHAFT UND GESELLSCHAFT contain the fundamental principles of a new sociological approach of immense significance; it was necessary to develop them carefully, to free their capsule formulations from inherent inclarities and to show their tremendously important implications. Or, as Schutz stated it retrospectively in 1959: "I was under the spell of Max Weber's work, especially his methodological writings. I recognized, however, very soon that Max Weber had forged the tools he needed for his concrete research but that his main problem, understanding the subjective meaning a social act has for the actor, needed further philosophical foundation" (1977: 41).

In this constructive yet critical fashion, Weber's statements became the starting points of Schutz's first scholarly undertaking: the development, in greatest possible clarity, of a theory of the sociology of understanding, including the pursuit of the hidden implication of its key terms and the investigation of the problems concealed in its original formulation. The search for "further philosophical foundations," however, was tantamount to the search for a viable subjective psychology of consciousness.

These decisions made, it remains doubtful that Schutz foresaw the full extent of the consequences they should have for him personally. He had posed himself a task which, in terms of his later thinking, should turn out to be his own great scholarly "plan for life." In the course of its ongoing pursuit, he should remain true to his starting intentions and thus to Weber; in the course of its execution, he should make a great number of originary contributions which should transform the whole of his work into a body of knowledge of its own character and originality: The Weberian sociology of understanding, eventually, became the Schutzian sociology of the life-world. This term, by the way, pays homage to the insights and inspirations Schutz gained from a few philosophers who had significantly occupied themselves with the psychological problems connected with the basic factors of human consciousness: Henri Bergson, Edmund Husserl, and William James. The "life-world" label for Schutz's mature sociology [2] makes use of Husserl's fruitful conception; but Schutz, under a more pedestrian title, had worked out by himself a quite comprehensive theory of the wide realm of social human experiences covered by it.

However, the present study focuses on the first phase of the realization of Schutz's scholarly life plan as precipitated in the unfinished manuscripts of his Bergson project.

Living in post-war Vienna, Schutz found himself exposed to contradictory tendencies: One was the rationalist-idealist tradition which had governed the thinking of his teacher generation and which he had accepted in his early academic training [3]. The other was contained in the intellectual climate prevailing among the young generation which, under the impact of the experiences of war and political-economic collapse, largely considered this tradition meaningless and, instead, resorted to psychoanalysis, esoteric literary cults, and/or philosophies of existentialism and the 'irrational.'

At the very outset of his search for philosophical foundations for his planned undertakings, Schutz followed the example of his teacher, Hans Kelsen, and scrutinized "the teaching of the neoKantian school." But he found that "neither the works of Cohen, Natorp, or the earlier writings of Ernst Cassirer opened to me an avenue of approach to the problem I was concerned with" (1977: 41). Thus, he felt compelled to seek such an avenue elsewhere. An alternative was offered to him by his closest friend, Felix Kaufmann.

Kaufmann, his elder by four years, had taken Schutz under his wings during his study years. A brilliant thinker, he was at home in Mathematics and Philosophy. He steered Schutz to the early phenomenological writings of Husserl, that is, the LOGICAL INVESTIGATIONS (1900-1901) and the first volume of the IDEAS. Schutz studied them "with the greatest care, but in spite of my great admiration I could not find in these books the bridge to the problems with which I was concerned." Instead, he decided to turn to Henri Bergson (1859-1941), whose ideas were best known under the name of Vitalism. Unlike most of the German-speaking enthusiasts of Bergsonianism at the time, Schutz became not a Vitalist. If he was immediately and deeply impressed by Bergson, so for more specific reasons: "I was convinced that his analysis of the structure of consciousness and especially of inner time could be used as a starting point for an interpretation of the unclarified basic notions of the social sciences, such as meaning, action, expectation, and first of all intersubjectivity" (1977: 42).

The conviction made him, the critical Weberian sociologist, to adopt simultaneously the stance of a critical Bergsonian philosopher. For more than four years, it should govern his scholarly efforts.

BERGSON SOURCES

When Schutz set out to write his first book, devoted to the clarification of the "basic notions of the social sciences," he refrained from naming any of the publications of Bergson which he was using for this purpose. But when he announced his intention "to retrace the path from the inner experience of pure duration to the concept of space," he made an exception by adding that he would do this "on hand of Bergson's conception, especially as formulated in his later writings" (1982: 33).

This is a startling hint, since the two earliest books of Bergson were definitely the most important for Schutz's project: the ESSAI SUR LES DONNEES IMMEDIATES DE LA CONSCIENCE (1889) and MATIERE ET MEMOIRE (1896). The latest book by Bergson available to Schutz was the essay collection DUREE ET SIMULTANEITE (1922, enlarged edition 1923). It contained mostly early articles on topics related to the ESSAI. It may have served Schutz as an access lane to the early books of Bergson. In DER SINNHAFTE AUFBAU, written a few years later, Schutz referred repeatedly to the 1923 edition of DUREE [4] and listed the seven main titles which appeared between 1889 and 1923 as sources. But, since he often quoted verbatim, it could be established that he worked essentially from the original edition of the ESSAI.

MAKING WEBER CONSISTENT

As pointed out, Schutz concentrated on Weber's sociology of understanding. The clarifications he sought were connected with the 'subjective' aspects of such a sociology and comprised two basic tasks. When Weber referred to the meanings social actors connect with their conduct, he took it for granted that they are beings endowed with consciousness, feeling, volition, intelligence, and the capacity to experience themselves, their actions, their surroundings. While, as sociologist, he was entitled to do so, his thematic questions called for pre-sociological investigations of the very subject matter of consciousness and what it entails. Correctly understood, such investigations were of a psychological nature, although not of the then new variety of experimental (natural-science) psychology, but rather of the old-fashioned kind as presented by philosophers from the British sensualists to the neoKantians and beyond [5]. What Schutz aimed at, was essentially nothing but what Edmund Husserl had developed and eventually labelled phenomenological psychology (1929). However, in order not to give the impression of rashly claiming thinkers like Bergson and James for Phenomenology, I have referred to their psychologies of consciousness - here and elsewhere - as to phenomenal psychologies. But I consider them akin to Husserl's phenomenological psychology at least in that they obtained their data from immediate introspective observations [6].

But Weber's sociology of understanding did not merely call for an appropriate underpinning by a corresponding psychology of consciousness, it also was directed upon the understanding of the "meaning meant" by the person with whom a social actor becomes involved during the course of interactional activities. With this, in Schutz's term of the time, the "Thou problem" was posed. Again, this question of the foundations and workings of intersubjective understanding did not occur by Weber, and again, Schutz was convinced that Weber's thematic inherently posed the question of the "Thou" and that, consequently, a serious attempt had to be made to answer it.

It was due to both the basically 'subjective' and 'intersubjective' presuppositions and implications of Weber's position that Schutz was led to mobilize the help of Bergson and to work out a theory of consciousness whose aspects he treated under the label of life forms and whose substantive content he defined as meaning structures.

APPROACH TO CHAPTERS 2 AND 3

THE BERGSON-SCHUTZ COMBINATION

The first chapter offered an introduction to the actual appraisal of Schutz's Bergson project. It is time now to face the substance of the study itself. The first item to be considered is the content of Bergson's psychology of consciousness in all those of its substantive and conceptual aspects which entered into Schutz's earliest work. The second task is to give a coherent outline of that theory which Schutz was building up on these foundations, and to convey a clear picture of the conceptual framework of his theory of life forms and meaning structure. These two tasks are attended to in chapters 2 and 3.

They were written by Ilja Srubar, the editor of the German documentary edition of the LIFE FORMS.

The second chapter, while departing from the core theme of Schutz's project, that of the Thou posed with the acceptance of Weber's sociology of understanding, enters directly into an exposition of the findings and conceptualizations which Schutz took over from Bergson. Thereby, the reader will gain a condensed yet clear picture of that phenomenal psychology which was one of the two main sources from which Schutz developed the theoretical ideas contained in the manuscripts of the LIFE FORMS.

The first part of the third chapter contains a factual exposition of Schutz's theoretical 'system' of the life forms, followed by a description of the individual life forms which, by Schutz, represented so many progressing layers of this 'system,' which amounted to a unique psychology of consciousness. In the chapters that follow, I have shifted the focus of my own expositions away from the theory of the life forms; instead, I concentrated on some of its inherent difficulties and, most of all, on aspects and tendencies in the manuscripts of the LIFE FORMS which had lasting effects on the post-Bergsonian development of Schutz's thinking and which I consider lasting contributions to the accumulation of knowledge which is the tangible backbone of the phenomenological movement. References to the theory of life forms, in these chapters, are accidental to these central purposes, and indicate original points of departure for Schutz's thinking whose eventual results can be accepted on their own terms. Therefore, the lengthy first part of the second chapter is the more significant for the reader who would like to know more about the theory of the life forms itself; he will gain a reliable picture in a more painless fashion from Srubar's exposition than he would when he tried to abstract it from the published Bergsonian manuscripts of Schutz.

The second part of the third chapter contains Srubar's positive appraisal of Schutz's achievements as embodied in his study of the LIFE FORMS. Needless to say, he touches upon various topics which I have discussed at length in the later chapters of this study. But, since he approaches them usually from a different angle and emphasizes different aspects, I consider his views not contradictory but complementary to mine. In addition, he has advanced quite original observations and interpretations of his own. I will mention here only one: his both challenging and convincing argument that Schutz's eventual decision to treat intersubjectivity as the exclusive affair of the life-world can be traced back to his early acceptance of Bergsonian ideas.

Readers will find considerable differences in style of tone of the bulk of Srubar's expositions and the bulk of my considerations. Next to unavoidable differences in background and personality, this is due to a simple factual reason. Where I am writing critical expositions under initial consideration of biographical and motivational factors, Srubar is bent on straight expositions of Bergson's and Schutz's reasoning; thus, he conveys a reliable picture of the theoretical content or gist of Schutz's Bergsonian studies. In fact, he offers a clear access to raw and in themselves complex drafts which otherwise would demand considerable more effort on the part of anyone who wishes to comprehend them. It is just this factuality which has allowed me to devote my own efforts essentially to discussions which presuppose a minimum of familiarity with the original manuscripts.

I can only hope that the combination of two separate efforts within the same covers is as beneficial for their readers as it was for me when I worked out my parts of this study.

TECHNICAL NOTES

Ilja Srubar tended to the translation himself. It was made for a by now obsolete common purpose. In view of the difficulties of inter-continental communication, we made an agreement to the effect that, on my end, no changes in the content of the selected chapters are made. However, I have made editorial changes in the structure of sentences which followed German syntax too closely and tried to adapt the text to American usage.

Where Srubar's translation of German technical terms differed from that used in the English edition of the LIFE FORMS, I have indicated this in footnotes preceded by my initials, HRW. Occasional annotations by me have been identified in the same manner. Unmarked footnotes to chapters 2 and 3 are those of Srubar.

The quotations from the manuscripts of the LIFE FORMS, which Srubar included into his expositions, were translated by him from the original German text. I replaced them by the formulations contained in the English edition which, in the meantime, has become available in print. Accordingly, the source identifications refer to this edition.

In addition, we have agreed that each author resumes full responsibility for the content of his chapters. Therefore, readers are advised not to make one responsible for what they consider flaws or errors in the chapters of the other.

CHAPTER 2

BERGSON'S CONTRIBUTION TO SCHUTZ'S PROJECT

by ILJA SRUBAR

The answer to the question of the meaning of the "Thou" arising from Weber's determination of social action had to be sought outside Weber's interpretative sociology; Weber, simply, had presupposed a meaningful relation between "I and Thou." "Extra-sociological tools" for this search offered themselves in Bergson's philosophy. Which of his concepts became a part of Schutz's thought?

Limitations of space make it impossible to offer even a synoptic overview of the thoughts of Bergson. I can sketch here only those ideas of his which left deep impressions on Schutz's theories of life forms and the structures of meaning. The influences of the following concepts are most clearly ascertainable:

(a) Durée as the inherent stream of lived experience and the externalized world-time as its symbolic representations;

(b) Memory as the location of meaningful organization of images of (past) experiences;

(c) The body as the center of our action (Taetigkeit) in the extensive world, as mediator between "world" and "I";

(d) Division of consciousness into a multiplicity of levels, denoted by durée, memory, and body as well as the "attention à la vie" which is connected with them as a differentiated moment;

(e) Differentiation between elapsed, elapsing, and planned movement [1].

In order to clarify the connection between the Bergsonian and Schutzian approaches, I will characterize each of these points.

(a) The I persists in the stream of coming-to-be and passing away of experiences. 'Durée' stands for the successive, continuous, and irreversible stream of our qualitative, non-spatial lived experiences in their diversity and heterogeneity for the original stream of the I

(1889: 174-175). [2] We 'reach' this original stream of time through profound reflection; it is not 'systematic' and it is possible only in "rare moments." The systematic analytical attempt at comprehending consciousness-in-durée transforms these rare glimpses into a series of static, fixed elements whose course of time is assumed to take place in a discontinuous "cinematographic" time -- that is, in geometric spatiality (line, point, parallel) (1889: 124-125, 138-139, 179). In reason inheres the capacity to undertake the isolation, fixation, and spatialization of lived experiences which elapse in the duration of the continuous I . Bergson called it symbolization. Spatialized, homogeneous, discontinuous and thus quantifiable time, then, is to be viewed as the external symbol of duree. The resulting spatialization and externalization of the continuing I [3] appears as a condition of its capacity to enter into social relationships. In this context, language is to be considered an instrument of symbolization; it enables the I to comprehend others by way of its apperception of realities (1889: 94 et seq 97-98, 125-126).

(b) Memory "incorporates the past into the present, draws many moments of the continuation of durée together into a single perception" (1896: 67). An experience, which has elapsed in duration, is seized and ordered by; it exists coextensively in consciousness (1896: 164). Memories in true memory, as such, 'exist' in the past and thus are neutral and possibly unconscious. Their coming-to-be in immediacy is brought about by the I that faces the necessity to adapt itself in each case to any currently specific situation. They are recalled because they are useful for the task to be carried out in the present (1896, pp. 158-159). To be sure, that means that lapsed memories to not remain the same. They are modified in the current context; but, in turn, they themselves modify this context. Therefore, no two experiences, necessarily belonging to different 'moments' in duration, could be alike (1896: 150-151). For contexts of experience to be perceived as such, it is necessary that they have expired: What is perceived is always the past. What appears "in the light of consciousness," always appears in relation to an actual situation. In the situation, "the immediate portion of the past ... is directed toward the future and ... works upon it in order to realize it ..." "Some of the light" falls "upon those conditions which lie further back in the past ... which comes into question for a useful connection with our present condition, that is, with our immediate past; the rest remains in darkness" (1896: 163). Thus, memory fulfills the two functions mentioned above, in which it assumes two forms. First, as true spontaneous consciousness-connected memory, it preserves lapsed experiences and makes perception possible. Secondly, as that which is bound to the memory of the organism, it enables us to react properly to a discrete current situation in that it selects associatively and recalls appropriate memories (1896: 64, 75 et seq.). Bergson refers to this second form also as the "memory of the corporeal organism"; it carries "pragmatic" references to the situation and points to the important role of corporeality in this connection.

(c) The body is the center of activity of the I in extended continuity - the world of space and time. It is the extensive form of the continuing I. It mediates between duration and the spatial-temporal world of extension and transposes memories into spatial acts (1896: 75). On the other hand, through it objects can act upon the experiencing I. At the same time, objects can be acted upon through the body - and this is fundamental for our perception (1896: 259-260). As center of our activities in the extensive world and bearer of perception, the body serves consciousness in any given moment as distinguishing medium. As such, however, the body represents only one of the levels of consciousness (1896: 150, 165, 268). In this sense, it is an "unalterable renascent part of our comprehension": it is its "always present portion." Indeed, the body is the bearer of perception and, as such, a "place of transition." In relation to consciousness, the body is no producer of thoughts but rather of standing ingredients of their actuality. "Itself an image, the body cannot store up images." Rather, it is a sensory-motoric "provider" of situation-related memories, although one which contributes nothing to their contents and their order in consciousness (1896: 164, 166, 251).

(d) Consciousness is to be seen as something divided into innumerable levels. Its division occurs through the various degrees of "_attention à la vie_"; they constitute the diverse possibilities of organization of our thoughts (1896: 184 et seq.). If memory is considered the location of the pragmatic organization of experience, the differences in the _attention à la vie_ produce innumerable possibilities of a stratification of memory; it can be imagined as being stretched out between two poles. They, in turn, can be imagined as states of the _attention à la vie_, ranging from the greatest to the least intensity. One pole can be viewed as the level of sensory-motoric corporeal tensions. The other is the level of "pure" memory and comprises all lived experiences of our duration; it makes them accessible to us as "pure images" - so, for instance, in dreams. Bergson envisioned as relevant future task but left aside the description of the system of thought-organization of the respective layers as well as the principles of the transition of thoughts from one layer of consciousness to another (1896: 183, 185).

(e) The concepts of _durée_, of symbolization, and of memory enabled Bergson to draw up a theory of action. He departed from the question of the freedom of action (1889: 109), and began by investigating to what degree an action is not free but determined. His criterion of determination is the predictability of actions on the basis of its known original motive. However, it appears that even a presentation of the totality of possible motives of an action, it itself, does not faithfully depict the characteristics of the execution of an act in its _durée_. Only in the coming-to-be and passing-away phases of action does it take its concrete form. Since no two experiences in their durée can be the same, the execution of the act is essentially free. Therefore, the assumed conditions of an action, as fixed cognitively and thus separated from the modified course of durée could never be adequate to the real motives and determine beforehand the course of action (1889: 141 et seq 151-152, 167-168). The real course of an action can be established only after it has been terminated. Having ceased, it can be symbolized in memory and thereby grasped as a "summarizing psychical datum." The following consequences emerge from this fact: (a) The essential difference between the time-modes of the act, that is, between expiring action and the future terminated action; (b) the distinction which results from this difference for the Ego in contrast to the Alter Ego with respect to their possible access to the real course of action. (c) If the Ego wishes to learn the reasons for its act, that is, to reconstruct its course in durée, it must by way of symbolization single out the expired act from its past durée and, thus, transpose it into space-time (1889: 151-152, 167-168). (d) If an Other wishes to predict an act of the I, he must as well deduce it from its motives. He can proceed either "dynamically" or "statically." Dynamically means here to attempt to establish exactly the succession of the phases of action which constitute the act in durée. The static proceeding accepts the act as completed beforehand and evaluates it according to conditions assumed to have prevailed at its origin. The effects of these conditions are considered invariable during the entire course of the action (1889: 142 et seq.)

In principle, the static variant is useless because the real course of an action is not predetermined; it, as well as its beginning and its end is formed only during its course in durée (see above). The dynamic approach is marked by difficulties of its own. A complete empathy with the durée of the Alter Ego is impossible; its assumption would mean the identity of two persons who are always different from one another - and that already in their bodies (1889: 144) [4]. Bergson did not treat this theme in detail but developed merely one variant of it in his argumentation against the deterministic prediction of actions. But he suggested a solution: Although the identity of two durations is impossible, our free actions express the past of the I and summarize it. Thus, an Alter Ego with a thorough knowledge of the past of an I could be in a position to empathize with the phases of a course of action in the durée (1889: 141-142).

With this, I have outlined the most important Bergsonian ideas which served Schutz during his construction of the theory of the Life forms [5].

CHAPTER 3

THE THEORY OF LIFE FORMS

by ILJA SRUBAR

THE LIFE FORMS AND THE STRUCTURE OF MEANING

Multi-Layer System of Consciousness: Bergson, as shown, refrained from a more exact definition of the strata of consciousness, their structuring, and their reciprocal relationships. In addressing these questions, Schutz saw the possibility of delineating the constitution of the "Thou." In Schutz's view, layers of consciousness become life forms: The I exists in their unity. Every life form, except the lowest one, corresponds to an organization of memory images peculiar to it. This organization amounts to a system of symbolization. It is possible to interpret the experiences of a lower life form within the symbol framework of the next-higher one. From here, Schutz developed Bergson's approach further. In order to clarify the constitution of meaning, as it occurs in acts of consciousness, Schutz had to analyze the process of symbolization much more exactly than Bergson had done.

Thus, Schutz set himself a dual task. First, the individual life forms must be specified. Second, the outline of a theory of symbolization must be established; it has to identify the characteristic system of symbolization (standing for a system of meaning) for each respective life form, without losing sight of the given context of the life forms in their mutual symbolic relationships.

In the manuscripts accessible to us, Schutz distinguished six such life forms in all [1]. I enumerate them here as they were listed in the theoretical part of LIFE FORMS AND MEANING STRUCTURE (1982: 52-53):

(a) the life form of pure duration of the I
(b) the life form of the memory-endowed duration of the I
(c) the life form of the acting I
(d) the life form of the Thou-related I
(e) the life form of the speaking I
(f) the life form of the conceptually-thinking I

The fundamental work for the theory under discussion had been undertaken in this first part. However, this manuscript breaks off after the analyses of the first three life forms. Fortunately, we are in the position to reconstruct the remaining life forms, at least in their essence, from the remaining manuscripts. For the life form of the Thou-relationship, all three of these manuscripts can be consulted; for the life form of the speaking I, "Meaning Structures of Language" and "Meaning Structures of Literary Art Forms" can be cited; for the life form of the conceptually-thinking I, we can again refer to the "Meaning Structures of Language."

I wish now to sketch briefly the theory of the life forms and their contextual meaning; subsequently, I will deal with the individual life forms.

If, with Schutz, one begins with the question of the meaning of the Thou-experience, one must investigate the possible approaches to this Thou and to the world in general which are at the disposal of the constituting I. These possible approaches are those stances of the consciousness of the I toward the world with Schutz calls the life forms (1982: 52-53). Like Bergson, Schutz assumed that there can be a multiplicity of life forms in the field of tension between the two poles of consciousness. However, Bergson delimited the tension-field of consciousness by the layer of "pure memory" on the one hand and that of the body on the other; Schutz placed it between the life form of pure duration and that of conceptual thinking.

Schutz's limiting terms are opposites determined by the realm of Bergson's dichotomy. The life form of pure duration is defined by the characteristics of quality, non-dimensionality, continuity, heterogeneity, freedom and memory "images," while the life form of conceptual thought is distinguished by spatio-temporality, quantifiability, extension, discontinuity, homogeneity, necessity, and conceptuality. Between these poles, a continuous series of life forms may be imagined. Of course, Schutz did not claim to have comprehended the entire continuum of life forms. He constructed the six enumerated life forms ideal-typically as heuristic tools for the purposes of his investigation, and he regarded the poles as limiting cases of a possible type of constitution (1982: 53). Each of the life forms contains its own system of symbolization, that is, a system of establishing meanings. With increasing distance from the life form of pure duration, these systems become ever more complex. A specific rule applies basically to the mutual relationship of symbol systems: the contents of experiences in a lower life form are explicable only within the scope of the next higher one. (We will see in the following how Schutz derived this rule.) A further principle applies: in spite of structural and substantial differentiations in the unfolding of particular symbol systems, their contents must be reducible to the primary original form of lived experiences in duration (1982: 56-57).

In the course of his analyses, Schutz worked out the structure of the symbol and meaning-constituted systems. It is common to all life forms; all assertions made about specific life forms must be compatible. He offered the following general rules [2] concerning the structure as a whole:

(1a) Symbol and symbolized are one in the awareness of the life form which precedes the symbol experience.

(1b) Symbol and symbolized are discrepant. This is mainly due to the difference between the points ascribed to them in the flow of duration. The symbolized passes into the symbol like becoming glides into passing-away.

(2) The symbolized (as having passed away) can be actually experienced only in the more primitive life form. In the present one it is symbol. For this reason, it is potentially experienceable. This means it 'becomes' within our inner duration.

(3) To turn to the symbol means to move in the direction of inner duration within a specific life form as totality of becoming. To inquire into the symbolized (that which is meant) means to search for that which has passed away in a different life form.

(4) In the same life form, every symbol interpretation is the positing of a symbol out of the Now and Thus which became a Thus by way of a preceding symbol positing of the same quality experience.

(5) Turning from the symbolized to the symbol, and vice versa, occurs in an act of consciousness which is characteristic for the given life form.

The transition from one life form to another occurs in a process of symbolization. For Schutz, this process meant the acts of singling out past living experiences from the continuous flow of duration and to reduce them analytically to limited units: symbols (1982: 55). What in the preceding life form appears as the experienced unity of that which is symbolized with the symbol is presented as mere symbol in the next higher one. The process of symbolization is always based on the relationship between at least two corresponding different life forms.

Lived experiences of a life form can enter into the respective higher one only through symbolization. If lived experiences XYZ of life form A have entered into life form B through symbolization, the Symbols Sx, Sy, and Sz are to be viewed as lived experiences of life form B, which again enter into life form C through symbolization, appearing there as Ssx, Ssy, and Ssz. The process of establishing symbols, at the same time, is also that of establishing meaning: According to the fourth point, the passed-away experiences in the lower life form, during the process of symbolization, are interpreted from the perspective of the given "now-and-thus" (1982: 57, 61). Consequently, as "meaning images" the symbols become bearers of the meanings of lived experiences. These experiences, as that which the symbol symbolizes, can now be reconstructed by directing attention to the previous lower life form in which the symbol was constituted. Thus, the life-form context of the symbol relationship is a meaning context. In this sense, the structure of the symbol order conditions every experience, for the concept of experience implies already a claim to meaningfulness which does not spring from this concept itself (1982: 70).

After this short sketch of the theory of the life forms and their structure of meaning, the individual life forms may be presented.

(a) The life form of pure duration of the I [3]: For Bergson as well as Schutz, pure duration represented the heterogenous, continuous, and irreversible flow of the lived experiences of the I, in which the originally lived qualitative experiences of the world flow continually into each other, become and pass away. Accordingly, the life form of pure duration is the region of immediate experiences; in them, the world is presented to us through complex lived experiences. The emotional and perceptual contents of these experiences are infinitely modulated. In the totality of their abundance, they are untransferable into the higher life form (1982: 31-32). Although there are higher forms of the mind which aim at transferring original experiences into higher forms of life - so music or lyric poetry (1982: 189-196, 162-163) - they must bow also to the general necessity and express original lived experience of quality through means which correspond to the extensive, spatial-temporal character of the external world. Yet, this world is presented to us in the mode of original experiences in a life form; this mode is distinguished radically from the world itself and from all other approaches to it: the mere reflection about the experiences 'made' in this life form cancels the peculiarities of its characteristic mode of experiencing reality. Thus, the questions arise: How is it possible to transfer qualitative lived experiences, representing the material for every constituting of meaning, from one life form to another one? How, above all, does the experiencing I relate to the extended spatial-temporal world?

When one envisions the goal of Schutz's study, the pressing need for answering these questions becomes clear. He wanted to clarify the meaning of the Thou-experience and, thereby, to develop interpretative sociology. Indeed, the Thou is given in the extended world. Therefore, it becomes necessary to "examine the means at our disposal for unifying in our consciousness the two realms of our existence: the experience of the I in duration and the Thou experience in space and time" (1982: 32).

We have already become acquainted with the process by which the experiences of one life form flows into another one: the process of symbolization. Now, I wish to describe that life form in which the first of these transfers takes place. I will indicate Schutz's answer to the question of the transference of lived experiences from pure duration into other life forms.

(b) The life form of the memory-endowed duration of the I: We do not find the idea of a memory-endowed duration by Bergson. However, it is a consequent continuation of the Bergsonian reflections about memory as the location of the "organization" of experience-images. Memory has a double function: First, of summing up and preserving lived experiences in the form of memory-images in their variety and succession; secondly, to make us conscious of them again, if required, as individually selected memories, singled out from duration. It cannot exist outside of or beside duration. Rather, it must be imagined as a component of duration itself. Memory is borne by duration especially in its first function. Duration, also, modifies its content.

Let us inspect the two functions of memory: In its first function, it produces a complete image of lived experiences in pure duration. It endures with us, "automatically" seizing every lived experience in the form of a memory-image and making us aware of our duration with its multitude of past living experiences. In this sense, it conditions our inner life. However, it does not seize the lived experiences themselves but rather the memory images which arise from the symbolization of original lived experiences. Memory does not preserve lived experiences by mirroring them; it transforms them into memory-images and interprets the elapsed lived experiences from the angle of the discrete "now-and-thus." Placing them into a context of previous and following lived experiences, it makes them into symbols (1982: 36-37, 38-39, 45-56, 38, 47-48). As symbol, the lived experience is not reproduced in duration. Rather, it occurs in its contextual meaning related to the given "now and thus." Further, the continuous becoming and passing-away of experiences in duration is cut by memory into limited units; these can become conscious as individual memory-images in the given "thus and now." This creates the possibility of separating individual lived experiences from the stream of duration and their further meaningful conversion in other life forms.

This conception of memory has two major consequences for the interpretation of the process of constituting meaning: In its experiences, duration is accessible only indirectly through memory. Simultaneously, the fixation of a lived experience in memory leads to its interpretation in the context of other - temporally adjacent - lived experiences. This context is an essential component of the symbol of the lived experience. However, in order to integrate a lived experience into such a context and to make it into a symbol, it is necessary that this experience be comprehensible as an entity; that is, that it be elapsed. That is why our experiences become only meaningful after they have passed away: "To ask about the meaning of an experience means to look for the place of an experience-having-past in the flow of pure duration. It means asking how a past experience of ours fits into the general line of our life" (1982: 48). In duration is no separate "thus-and-now" allowing one to relate to elapsed lived experiences. Experiences in the immediate process of becoming in pure duration are meaning-free [4]. They receive meaning and become interpretable only when they are isolated through a retrospective act of apprehension. The symbolizing function of memory allows lived experiences to enter higher life forms as that which is being meaningfully experienced (1982: 72).

I now wish to trace, with Schutz, the question of the relationship of the experiencing I in duration to the spatial-temporal world. He provided us with an answer in his analysis of the next life form.

(c) The life form of the acting I: The experiencing I in duration is not immaterial, incorporeal. The awareness of the unity of the experiencing I includes the lived experience of its body as essentially belonging to him. The lived experience of this distinguishes my body from all other bodies in the world. How does this experience come about?

Proceeding from duration, my own body is presented to me in a dual manner: First, I have acoustical and optical qualitative lived experiences of my body (for example, my clapping hands); second, there is what Schutz called "the somatic feeling of life." Under it fall the lived experiences of my body in motion. If these two groups of experience are viewed as appearing in duration, they cannot coincide: In duration, nothing is simultaneous but all is in continuous flux. Such life experiences do not suggest meaningful associations between sensory and kinesthetic experiences, even if such association is symbolically conceivable in memory-endowed duration. In the realm of memory endowed duration, a coincidence of optical and kinesthetic lived experiences of a bodily movement may be certifiable. But this is not a sufficient basis for securing the paramount position of embodied experiences [5]. Necessarily, they are a new kind of experience belonging to another life form - one which carries in itself the evidence of my body's "belonging-to-me." This function belongs to the "somatic feelings of life"; through them, kinesthetic muscle tensions are experienced as belonging to me even before their reconstruction in memory-endowed duration (1982: 79-80).

This evidence is given only if it is borne by a kinesthetic experience, that is, only when the body is in motion; so, if the I acts. The body is only experienceable in its functions and thus in a functional context. Awareness of the continuing identity of my body as something belonging to me and always accompanying me, accordingly is only possible through symbolizing acts of memory. Corporeality, thus constituted, therefore cannot be the basis of the original I-identity (1982: 81, 101).

Nevertheless, I experience my body in its movements and actions in the world. I experience these movements and actions of my body as presently elapsing in duration on the one hand, and as terminated and localizable in the spatial-temporal world on the other (1892: 94). With this I-experience as well as through the sense of touch, the demarcation line between my body and the world is drawn. It is at the same time that between my body and its environment. Through the lived experience of this delimitation the I can experience itself, so to say, as viewed from the outside. This experience backs up the reconstructed unity of my body as symbolized in my consciousness as an extended substance, as a body in space. The capability of the I to perform this symbolization is characteristic of the life form of the acting I; it provides us with an access to the world of extension. Since it carries corporality and somatic feelings of life, it includes the extensity of the spatial-temporal world in duration (1982: 87-88). Thus, the milieu of the acting I - the spatial-temporal world of objects - is in its materiality and objectivity coupled to the experiencing and acting I. What for the I is the evident objective materiality of the data of the spatial-temporal world, originates in the I's intercourse with these data themselves. The life form of the Acting I produces the break-through to the world (1982: 105, 108).

With the life form of the acting I, the relationship to the spatial-temporal world is established. In it, the Thou presents itself as well; its meaningful constitution is an essential subject matter of investigation. Unfortunately, Schutz's study breaks off at this point. Thus, I will have to consult the remaining manuscripts for the reconstruction of the other life forms.

(d) The life form of the Thou-related I: Schutz went beyond Bergson already in his theory of symbols and life forms. With the analysis of the Thou-relationship, he entered a new thematic area; its foremost characteristic is the turn to sociological questions. The focus of Schutz's analysis, now, is the possibility of the meaningful comprehension of the Thou and of the meaning established by it. Thus, he addressed the problem of intersubjectivity, postulated as a fundamental theme of interpretative sociology. As noted before, the problem has two components which are coupled together: First, there is the meaningful comprehension of the Thou as alter ego; second, there is the understanding of the meaning established by this Thou [6]. In his investigation of the life form of the speaking I, he treated the second moment predominantly. Yet, he also made important statements about the situational conditions of the intersubjective understanding of meaning independent of language. I would like to include them in my presentation of the life form of the Thou-related I. First, I will turn to Schutz's investigation of the possibility of the meaningful understanding of the Thou.

In the life form of the acting I, experience is anchored in the spatial-temporal world of extensive things. The experience of the difference between the I and its environment, as given with one's body, allows to project lived-experiences-passing-away-in-duration into the spatial-temporal world and to interpret them meaningfully by means of symbolization (1892: 105). The world comes into the field of vision on the level of the acting I; it is extensive and displays this in every thing existing outside of myself which can be subjected to meaningful interpretation. From this position, Schutz made the transition to the Thou-attitude:

> Among the things thus created, a series distinguish themselves which are related to my body in still another manner than merely by superficial and external similarity - that is, by extension in space and time. In outline and movement these objects are similar to my body and thus awaken special attention. Most of all, they stand out because they can be compared to the memory images of my own past I. Toward them, I assume the same most specific stance which I assume toward my own past I. In one word, they are consociates about whom I possess a quite primary knowledge. And now, a new symbol relation realizes itself, the third. I experience the Thou as if it too experiences a duration which in course and direction is similar to, nay, simultaneous with, mine; as if it possesses a memory which executes similar or maybe the same functions as mine. (I witness, HRW) its movement as if it is not merely movement like that of any other similar thing aside from me, but action - that is, movement which is accompanied by the characteristic phenomena of will and imagination which occur together with my specific bodily movements. Still more: I interpret the symbol which I impute to this object called 'Thou' as if its, and my, duration display a kind of parallelity, nay, as if the contents of experience in its duration enter into mine. The Thou stands at the intersection of two durations, two memories, two courses of action; mine, of which I have primary knowledge, and those which I interpret as my experiences of him.
>
> This symbol relation leads me to presuppose that the same experience which I have of the Thou the Thou has of me. I accept the Thou as being understandable by me and as being able to understand me and my life. Thus, I assume that I can posit actions which have a chance not only to be observed but

> also interpreted by the Thou. And I assume that I am able to comprehend movements of the Thou as his actions which, in turn, I can interpret in the manner in which I interpret my own actions. In this way, the space-time world, apparently created by my acting I, has been significantly changed and animated. ... The act of positing meaning by the Thou - the meaning interpretation by my I - this is the total enrichment of my world. Yet, it is merely the starting point for all my relations with Thou and thing, with world and surrounding. ...
>
> I have created the Thou in space and time already in the life form of the acting I. However, it will not exist as long as I confirm its existence only out (of the perspective, HRW) of my own life and not also out of the course of the life of the Thou (1982: 127-128) [7].

Obviously, we have here the earliest version of Schutz's "general thesis of the alter ego" which is fundamental for his conception of intersubjectivity. He presents the Thou as another subject experienced in duration.

However, how is the meaning understood which is symbolized in the Thou's actions? It is clear that it must be understood if I wish to receive a confirmation of my world by the Thou. In what form can such a confirmation take place? Answering this question implies a presentation of conditions which allow an intersubjectively established interpretation of the symbols of "Thou" and its actions. In the passages cited we find an essential hint, which Schutz systematically explained in DER SINNHAFTE AUFBAU: The I interprets the symbolized lived experiences of the Thou as if they were its own. But what brings about the probability of a correspondence between the meaning established by the Thou and my interpretation?

The solution of this problem presented itself indirectly to Schutz. Analyzing various art forms, he arrived at the interpretational context in which a spectator (or reader) of a drama or novel relates to this work itself. The general problem, here, is how the meaning objectivized in the work, as established by the artist, can be adequately interpreted.

Schutz's statements concerning the art form of the drama reveal the general possibility of understanding meanings established by the Thou. Here, Schutz's thesis was that, on the stage, the drama represents Thou relationships through symbolization (1982: 184-188, 185, 186, 196). He considered the manner in which the Thou-relationship, based on experiences of my and your durations, is transposed into symbols. He showed that symbolization, here on the state, is based on the transposition of that which is experienced in duration into a spatial-temporal situation: "The symbolization of inner duration is made solely possible by this transplantation into the world of space and time. No other art form can bring it so vividly before our consciousness as the drama - even though its means are apparently the extreme opposite of pure duration; they are of purely spatial-temporal and conceptual nature." Actions on the stage, aside from their linguistic expression, are understandable; they occur in a spatial temporal order. This order does not need to correspond to actual-life situations: Essential "it is not being-real but being taken for real. This alone creates the possibilities for all action and sensory impressions. Whether the room exists, or whether the acting person assumes it to exist, makes no difference: The room becomes surrounding, place of action, object of my acting, cause of my sensory impressions" (1982: 186, 188).

The impression of the reality of stage actions is created by their distinct arrangement in a spatial-temporal matrix. This gains importance also in other respects. The understandability of the action of an other and of the spatial-temporal order in which it takes place, depends here and in actual life on typification. The "possibilities of situations" which are under certain spatial-temporal conditions, can be subsumed under definite sets of types: "But this typification is not exhausted by time, space, and causality. The Thou-relation itself and the individual oriented toward it are typified; thereby, they become more general yet more individual" (1982: 188).

Schutz started here with the idea that the understanding of meanings established by the Thou is only possible by the simultaneous comprehension of the spatial, temporal, and social typicality of the situation in which the meaning of the Thou-relationship is symbolized. In his analysis of the art form of the opera, Schutz declared expressly that the comprehension of music as an expression of the duration of an alter ego is made possible only through the temporalization (Verzeitlichung) of the melody by rhythmization (1982: 193). This shows again that, at the time, Schutz thought that the intersubjective understanding of symbolizations, as established by the Thou, is carried by a temporality not exclusively belonging to individual duration but being also and necessarily supra-individual.

These conceptions have been derived from an analysis of symbolization in the realm of specific art forms. To what extent can they be generalized? We have seen in the treatment of the propositions about the symbol structure of the life forms that all symbol systems rest upon a common structure. Within it, they must be traceable to basic experiences in pure duration. This rule also applies to the analysis of the establishment and interpretation of symbols in the realm of art. Treating the problem of the relationship of the artistic symbol to the symbol systems of everyday life, Schutz wrote: "In spite of all transformations, the meaning of the final symbolic formulation must be identical with that of the original experience. Otherwise, no possibility would remain for meaningfully integrating these symbol series themselves, as experiences, into the stream of our consciousness" (1982: 172). Since this postulate applies generally, typifications of the temporal, spatial, and social dimensions of the establishment of symbols, under all circumstances, are indispensable for understanding meanings posited by the Thou. Intersubjectively established typifications, on which the understanding of Thou-posited meanings depends, belong in their majority simultaneously to language. Thus we have reached the fifth life form, that of the speaking I.

(e) The life form of the speaking I : An adequate consideration of this life form requires a modification of perspective. Analyzing the Thou-relationship, I still could proceed from the respective I to whom Thou-posited symbols are offered for interpretation. Thus, so to say, I could describe the Thou-relation as unidirectional. But, in the investigation of the life form of the speaking I, it is necessary to preserve the bipolarity of conversation. In this life form, the positer of meaning - the speaker - and the interpreter of meaning - the listener - are unavoidably linked to one another. This relationship is the first essential point of Schutz's investigation of this area. Language itself, as bearer of objectified contexts of meaning, comes next: it serves as a medium to which the I and the Thou relate jointly. A third point is the relationship of the elements of language - the words - to the fundamental experiences lived in duration.

It seems best to begin the presentation with Schutz's analysis of the objectifying character of language. He wrote: "The sphere of language is a life form of Man who lives in space, time and Thou-relation. In it occurs the highest transformation and symbolization of that which is experienced in pure duration" (1982: 160). The "symbolization" occurs in the process of naming (Namensgebung); in it, lived experiences are "typified and generalized" by way of the "conceptual-symbolic function of language." Through naming, "the thing and its character, the affect and its intensity, the action and its course" are "completely removed from the sphere of my specific experiences." "In language, I do not encounter experiences but solely formulae, patterns which, in their manner, can make my experiences communicable." The language-pervaded world is not that which I have experienced in duration, but in the first place in space and time. It depends neither on me nor Thou; it has created a "ghostly" and "truly unreal world." However, the separation of the "anonymous" word from that which is experienced allows to establish conceptual thinking and knowledge. In a sense, it mediates between the forms of lived experiences and of science (1982: 143, 129-131).

However, to provide scientific objectivity is not the exclusive function of language. In the life form of the speaking I, language is chiefly a bearer of typifications which serve symbolization in daily life. In this context, one can consider language an accessible "neutral" system of symbolization for everyone. But how comes the intersubjectivity [8] of the word to pass? Schutz named two essential conditions which determine the intersubjective character of linguistic typifications. On the one hand, it originates in the assigning of names through which the lived experience of the I is necessarily associated with the experiences of the Thou and, thereby with that of everyone else. On the other hand, it rests in the fact that I intend with the same word the same object, within the course of my duration, which you intend in yours: Thereby, the word gains trans-temporality, trans-spatiality, trans-individuality. It remains the same even though the symbolized time-and-space-bound object changes" (1982: 143).

Although language, in this light, is supra-individual, it is still bound to the subjects who use it. In the life form of the speaking I, which is erected on that of the Thou-relationship, linguistic usage singles out "the thing experience, with all its corresponding actual and potential characteristics, from the duration of the speaker and its integration into the duration of the listener." This indicates that speaking, respectively listening, individuals never actually proceed only from the "supra-individuality" and neutrality of linguistic symbols, but always place them in the given context of their durations. For this reason, the understanding of meanings expressed by the Thou in linguistic symbols also presents an approximation to that which is meant. Of course, it must be supported by extra-linguistic components in an intersubjective context, as mentioned before (1982: 146, 161-162).

How comes about this interaction between the positor and the interpreter of meaning? The positing of meaning occurs in the duration of the speaker; Schutz designates it as subjective meaning. By contrast, symbols to be interpreted as meanings posited by others stand in an objective - here linguistically fixed - context. According to Schutz, the act of positing meaning contains two elements. First, a relationship between the objective meaning context of language and the subjectively experienced contents of the planned communication must be established. Therewith, the selected words receive a specific subjective meaning for the speaker: he assimilates neutral words. Second, these assimilated linguistic elements must be formed into a "subjective meaning-endowed context of speech." Accordingly, every communication contains a selection of elements of the neutral linguistic materials related to the subjective contents which are to be communicated, but also the arrangement of these linguistic elements in the subjective meaning context of their oral presentation. The listener acts similarly but in reverse: He "integrates that which has been communicated to him and ... interprets it in terms of the objective meaning context of the given language material. From here, he pursues the context of the speech he has heard: ... he tries to understand the meaning which the speaker meant" (1982: 161).

However, the second step of the subjectivation of the statement heard by the listener is perceived only analytically by an uninvolved observer. For the listener, the word heard always stands in an objective meaning context.

This specification of the life form of the speaking I is as yet incomplete. The initiation of communication takes place with two intentions: that of eliciting understanding and that of evoking a reaction based on this understanding, regardless of whether the reaction is expressed in an action or in emotions (1982: 167). In this context, language is not only an intersubjective system of symbolization, it is also a part of the context of motivation and acting of the persons involved in a Thou relationship. By the same token, these contexts provide the linkage between linguistic symbolizations and that which is subjectively experienced.

(f) The life form of the conceptually-thinking I : The transition to this life form emerged clearly in the foregoing expositions. As a system of intersubjective symbolizations, language represents a system of neutralized objectivations of subjective lived experiences, comprehensible by everyone but independent of all. As means of communication, by contrast, it is used for establishing meanings and interpretations and thus is linked to subjective meanings and, ultimately, to personal duration. Schutz called this mediating function of linguistic typifications "the mystery of language." In the life form of the speaking I, it functions in its total complexity. However, the life form of the conceptually-thinking I rests upon its objectivizing moments independent of subjective meaning. Conceptual thought, the highest life forms of all, is the sphere which is most removed from the stream of lived experiences in duration. Its goal is objective knowledge (1982: 130).

I do not think that it can be said with certainty whether Schutz limited this life form to scientific thought or whether he included the general concepts of everyday life as well [9]. The core of his argumentation was a critical discussion of logic - the classical science of conceptual thought. The depth of his analysis of the foundations of logical thought and, above all, the congeniality of his and Husserl's argumentation [10] are worth a separate investigation; I will only note them here. In order to appraise the influence of Schutz's work in this period on his later studies, I wish here to treat the relationship between lived experiences, languages, and concept.

The problem here, again, is that of establishing meaning and interpretation. In contrast to the sphere of speech in the Thou-relationship, the nomenclature of conceptual formulations has an opposite effect: "The conceptual formulation of that which has been named offers the latter for interpretation as something completely objective without reference to the act of positing meaning and to that which is subjectively meant. The named object ... is here transformed into a class while the qualities of the object ... become criteria of the concept" (1982: 146).

Now, a question has to be posed: Is the sense of the arrangement of such concepts exhausted in their logical structure, or does it have another source? Schutz wrote: "For us, subject matter of consideration is not the proposition which had been developed out of concepts but the spoken sentence, bound to experience and Thou" (1982: 152) [11].

... The symbolizations of this life form are abstract concepts. If they are to make sense [12], they must be traceable to symbolizations of a lower kind: to the linguistic typifications of the life form of the speaking I or, as Schutz also said, to those of daily life. Their intersubjective meaningfulness is based upon the objectivation of experiences in the Thou-relation. Thus, concepts in a logical statement relate to reality not by virtue of their logical order in the sentence but through their relation to the reality of lived experiences in duration. And this relation is mediated by their linguistic - and thus re-subjectivizable - character [13].

Without this, abstract concepts and logical statements would be meaningless [14].

EVALUATION

The purpose of the foregoing presentation of the theory of the life forms was not only to present Schutz's line of reasoning but also to enable the reader to verify my conclusions. What follows is an attempt at locating in the Bergsonian manuscripts constructive components for Schutz's later work as well as pointing out theoretical decision he doubtlessly made concerning the solution of problems posed here. The attentive reader may not require such a list. However, since in my presentation I remained as close as possible to Schutz without comments, a short evaluation of the materials appears to be in order.

Obviously, the theory of the life forms contains some conceptions which determined later arguments by Schutz. Without claiming to have covered all of them, I selected the following as being of importance for the entire work of Schutz:

(a) the egological approach

(b) the reflexive constitution of meaning

(c) the foundation of intersubjectivity in the parallel durations of ego and alter ego

(d) The temporal, spatial and social dimensions of the social world and the pragmatic access of the individual to it

(e) Language

(1) as bearer of objectivized lived experiences
(2) as component of the interaction-context
(3) as mediator between lived experience and concept; the necessity to explore the prescientific mode of constitution of the world
(4) language and concept: objectivizations and second-order concept: objectivizations and second-order constructs

(a) The egological approach: Schutz's point of departure issued from the necessity to specify better the Weberian concept of subjective meaning as related to acting [15]. Weber's formulation of the problem left great leeway for interpretation. He did not determine whether the Other, as co-actor, participated in the constitution of meaning, or whether he is merely present as a 'point of reference' in need of interpretation. If this ambiguity is viewed through the lens of Bergson's conceptions of personal duration and memory, the preferability of an egological position becomes clear.

The question of subjective meaning, as established by the Thou, can be answered only through the constitutive performances of consciousness. Only when I have analyzed the process of the constitution of meaning in my consciousness can I say how I constitute that meaning which is established by the Thou. The egological analysis does not proceed solely from the fact that I have no direct access to the consciousness of others. Posing this question, I am asking about the meaning of the Thou and its actions. Thus, it becomes necessary to inquire how the meaning posited by the Thou becomes interpretable by me. Of course, the Thou in the Thou-relation takes part in the constitution of the world. But this occurs always in the manner in which the I receives a confirmation of its meanings and interpretations as established by the Thou. The common constitution of the world is not based on current, creative interaction, but primarily on the experience that the I and the Thou constitute the world in the same manner, so to say, parallel to one another. Thus, Weber's problem was solved through the application of Bergson's philosophy - long before Schutz accepted Husserl - in favor of a rigorous egological approach. The problem of intersubjectivity, playing no explicit role by Bergson, stands at the center of Schutz's endeavors.

(b) The reflective constitution of meaning: Weber did not determine the mode of the constitution of the meaning of an action. He left it open whether it is based on a deliberate project or issues in spontaneous reaction. The acceptance of Bergsonian theorems forced Schutz here also to make important decisions. Access to lived experience - the basis and material of our meaning-constitution - is only possible through singling them out and fixing them in memory. This act of apprehension can take place only after the lived experience has passed away in duration. Since fixation of lived experiences is the condition of symbolizations and thus of establishing meanings, constituting meaning is possible only retrospectively. Therefore, meaning does not belong to the ongoing action by only to the elapsed act. If I wish to turn to the Thou in order to act meaningfully, I must let my future act pass through my mind in all its phases. I allow it to elapse anticipatorily and thus become aware of its meaning. For this reason, for example, Schutz had to define the purpose of communication as that of evoking a reaction in the listener - as purposive-rational in Weber's sense - that is, calculated in advance (1982: 167). Bergson's concepts of durée and memory suggested to Schutz the transfer of all constitutional operations of consciousness to the province of the reflecting consciousness. Thus, from a certain level on, he equated its intentionality with its discursiveness: The meaning of a lived experience can only be constituted by reconsideration; thus, it has the character of ex post predication [16].

Under the influence of Bergson, Schutz developed a conception of meaning which was decisive for his entire work. It enabled him to make the viable alternative of Weber's interpretation his own. To repeat: The meaning of an action which explicitly turns toward the Thou, is only conceivable when presented as terminated. Accordingly, it rests on a deliberate project. This follows from the inherent logic of Schutz's theoretical 'system' of reasoning [17].

(c) The foundation of intersubjectivity in the parallel durations of ego and alter ego: As shown, the egological approach, which results from Bergsonian premises for treating the problem of meaning, raises urgently the question of intersubjectivity. Schutz's answer, designed with the aid of Bergson, here too presents a conception which, in his later work is not abandoned albeit supplemented. To convince oneself of this, he need only compare the best-known versions of the general thesis of the alter ego in AUFBAU (1932: 107, 112-113) [18] and in the COLLECTED PAPERS (CP I: 173-174) to the cited earlier draft. In the AUFBAU, intersubjective relations are anchored in the parallelity of two durations within dyadic relationships. Thereby, Schutz indicated the decisive step of a transition to the social world. The genesis of this step sheds more light on the noticeable difference between the intersubjectivity theories of Schutz and Husserl. Above all, the issue here is the role of "embodiment" in the constitution of an intersubjective relationship. In Husserl's "fifth meditation," embodiment determines decisively the identity of the ego in the primordial sphere (1931: 128): One comprehends the difference between "my body" and the constitutum "the body of the alter ego." Husserl sought to demonstrate an intersubjective relationship which does not have the character of a mere projection of ego's own consciousness into the alter ego -- which is to be constituted as an ego alien to me. Rather, he sought it in primordial immanence which contains a transcending intention pointing to the alter ego as apprehended in the body of the other (1931, sections 44, 45).

In the AUFBAU, Schutz did not make use of Husserl's construction; in the essay on intersubjectivity, he rejected it explicitly (CP III: 81). Having started out from the conception of duration and the necessity to locate all constitutive operations of consciousness in the sphere of its reflective acts, he cannot accept Husserl's construction. The body, whose essential mode is the "somatic feeling of life," appears only in the actuality of lived experiences. Thus, the body is not independent of but a component of all immediate fundamental experiences. It cannot be the bearer of the identity of the I; it must have been first reconstructed in memory-endowed duration. Rather, I-identity is founded in fundamental lived experiences in pure duration; these experiences are basic for all acts of consciousness. That means: The necessary differentiation between the streams of consciousness of the I and Thou cannot be derived from the difference between my body belonging to my primordial sphere and the body of an alter ego, but rather from the difference between the streams of consciousness themselves. What we termed above "reflective constitution of meaning," becomes apparent here. According to it, the differentiation between the two streams of consciousness results from the fact that the I can become aware of the lived experiences in its duration only retrospectively while it grasps those of the Thou in the actuality of their becoming.

Here appears a paradox [19]: The same philosophical premises which guided the analysis of the essential role of corporeality in the life form of the acting I plays in the constitution of the spatial-temporal world, also deny that the same corporeality plays any role in the reconstruction of the Thou-relationship in which the subjective constitution of the world is to be verified.

(d) The temporal, spatial, and social dimensions of the world and the I's pragmatic approach to them: Schutz accepted the thesis that lived experiences in duration must be established for others in a spatial-temporal objective form. This led him to the conclusion that the spatial-temporal order, as the frame of symbolization, is essential for the understanding of established meanings. But the Thou-relationship, based on the parallelity of two durations, is just as essential for securing the possibility of intersubjectively objectivized meanings and their conceptualization. Thus, Schutz posed a problem which entered his later investigations of the temporal, spatial, and social dimensions of the life-world. Time, Space, and Thou-relationship are not seen as simple dimensions in which the extended world appears; rather, they are extra-individual bearers of the conceptualized meaning of situations. These typifications allow to grasp meanings established with their help. Therefore, intersubjectivity is not only based on the parellelity of two durations in the sense of understanding in principle.

Situationally, it is also carried by the temporal, spatial, and social conditions under which meanings are established.

The conception of the ego's pragmatic relationship to the world was taken over from Bergson. It receives here a new component. I have shown, in the section on memory-endowed duration, that the meaning of lived experiences is constituted by arranging elapsed experiences into the context of past series of experiences from the vantage point of the given Now-and-Thus. This entails the pragmatic relationship of the I to the given situation. Proceeding from Schutz's statements about typifications related to time, space, and the Thou-relationship, we see that these are dimensions which are conceivable as typifications determining the given Now-and-Thus. The pragmatic relation is a situational one; it is essentially concrete. If we consider Schutz's description of the structure of the realm of everyday life, for example as given in the STRUCTURES OF THE LIFE WORLD [20], the temptation is strong to see the germ of this analysis in these early reflections.

(e) Language: In his first investigations of language, Schutz provided a whole series of starting points which gained greatest relevance in his later work. I wish now briefly to address those which seem to be most important.

(1) Language as bearer of objectivized lived experience: Schutz considered language a system of symbolizations of supra-individual character. At the same time, he considered linguistic symbols as objectivations of contents of the respective streams of lived experience in duration. The acts of assigning names, in which these objectivations occur, are the generalization, schematization, and typification of experienced contents. In the life-form of the speaking I, individuals use words as prefabricated typifications. Their content is intersubjectively fixed as sedimentation of common experiences of the 'same' objects. As described above, words are subjectivized when assimilated, that is, they are related to that which is subjectively experienced in order to express their subjectively constituted meanings. In this, language functions as bearer of inter-subjective typifications which, in the life form of the speaking I, belong to the province of "daily life." The conception arising here appears later to have entered into the essential determination of language as the "bearer of typifications in the province of everyday life" (1973: 233-235).

(2) Language as component of the interactional context: In the manuscript of "Meaning Structures of Literary Art Forms," Schutz analyzed the relationship between positing and interpreting meanings. In this frame, another conception appeared which should become permanently important to him: the connection between the motivating communication of the I and the corresponding reaction to it by the

Thou. Later, he expressed the same idea in the thesis of the "reciprocity of motives" (CP I: 23). Earlier, he established the context of action in speech acts and corresponding reactions; later, he conceived it in a generalized form as reciprocity of interactional expectations. Eventually, he elevated his analysis of the basic motivational relationships from the linguistic level to that of social interaction in general. Another important point came here to light: Through the inclusion of linguistic symbolizations in the motivational context of interaction, Schutz opened the way to an integration of action and linguistic communication.

(3) Language as mediator between lived experience and concept; the necessity to explore the prescientific constitution of the world: Schutz designated language as a "third realm" between the world of lived experience and that of concepts. It is independent of but mediates between both (1982: 152). What form does this relationship take? Language represents an objectivation of lived experiences; yet, as spoken lnguage of the speaking I, it stands as well in the subjective meaning-context of the concrete Thou-relationship. The concept lacks relation to concrete subjective meaning-contexts which would affect its objectivity. In comparison with duration, which represents the concrete abundance of that which is subjectively experienced and the diversity of the world, linguistic objectivation is a restriction of this variety. ... The concept represents the highest attainable reduction of this diversity; according to its 'nature,' it is separate from the subjective. Thus, it cannot be a primary expression of reality; and pure conceptual analysis (as that of logic) misses the reality of the world altogether. Hence, according to Schutz, it is necessary to investigate the I within the pre-logical or, as he said, the "alogical" attitude in which the "real" meaning of the world is constituted. This does not mean that concepts would lose their objectivity and scientific relevance because they are contentless or inadequate. They are bound to the concrete world through their linguistic form in its dual character. This form, on the one hand, received its intersubjectivity from the parallelity of durations of several egos; on the other hand, having become supra-individual, it represents a system of objectified lived experiences. The complete desubjectivation of these experiences occurs in the concept.

The Schutzian conception of a scientifically adequate access to the social world is expressed in this line of thought. Its fundamental meaning will become clearer in the further discussion of the relationship between language and concept.

(4) Language and concept; constructions of the first and the second order: When I speak here of constructions of the first and the second order, it might seem that I have read too much into the texts on hand. However, it can be shown that we are here at the source of the characteristics of Schutz's later methodological procedure. As

shown previously, one point of Schutz's analysis of the symbol relationship asserts: that which is symbolized is experienceable only in the life form preceding that of the symbolization. This means that all symbolizations, according to their content, are ultimately traceable to basic lived experiences in duration. This applies to all symbols. However, linguistic symbolizations occupy a special position: they represent the first stage of the objectivation of lived experiences; in the life form of the speaking I, they are to be seen as supra-individual typifications. Falling into the realm of daily life, these typifications are based on the parallelity of the durations of ego and Thou. Accordingly, the word is the primary objectivation of lived experiences on a supra-individual level: a primary typification of an intersubjectively sedimented meaning-context. Its usefulness as symbol hinges on its adequacy to experiences in duration (1982: 152, 172). Concepts are further objectivations of linguistic symbolizations. Their usefulness as symbols is based ultimately on lived experiences in previous life forms, that is, on experiences the producer or user of concepts has had of words as objectivations of the first order. Thought through, this means that a relationship of adequacy must exist between linguistic objectivations in the life form of the speaking I and concepts: that is, between objectivations of the first with such of the second order. Thus, we have to conclude that pertinent early investigations of Schutz were of decisive importance for his later methodological thinking.

CLOSING REMARKS

At the conclusion of these considerations, I will pose two questions. They cannot be answered here in detail but must at least be addressed: The influence of Bergson on Schutz and the originality of Schutz's thinking; the relationship of Schutz to Husserl.

In the light of the expositions offered here, there can be no question of Schutz's mere application of Bergsonian ideas. Schutz took over the basic dichotomy of Bergson's interpretation of the world. However, he creatively developed the concepts taken over from Bergson. Where did Schutz go beyond Bergson? I will enumerate only thematic areas in which Schutz developed his own approach. He had to work out for himself the description and analysis of the particular life forms as well as theory of symbol and meaning establishment. In the greater part of the essays concerning language, intersubjectivity, and Thou-relation, Schutz used Bergsonian premises in order to solve problems which had become relevant for him as a result of his orientation towards the social sciences. These efforts were thematically independent from Bergson.

Why, for the most part, did Schutz later replace the tools provided by Bergson with those developed by Husserl? H. R. Wagner suggested one plausible intrinsic reason for Schutz's eventual decision to abandon the

LIFE FORMS: Its Bergsonian framework did not allow him to achieve an unbroken analysis of the constitution of meaning (1977: 197-198). Only Husserl's investigations of internal time-consciousness and parts of his FORMAL AND TRANSCENDENTAL LOGIC (1928, 1929a) should give him access to the self-evidence of things which was missing in Bergson's durée pure. Seemingly, Husserl's conceptual precision was overwhelming; it largely drove out Bergson's terminology (apart from the conception of duration). But Schutz did not completely convert to Husserl's philosophy. The approaches and, above all else, the problems which the young Schutz had worked out should also dominate his future thinking. Thus, he continued to elaborate some problem complexes with the help of Bergson's theories; he resorted to them just in cases in which, in his judgment, the structure of Husserl's system exhibited rents and his transcendental constructions were at an impasse. Thus, Schutz applied his conception of intersubjectivity, devised with the help of Bergson's concept of duration, at that juncture in AUFBAU at which Husserl's transcendental aspirations blocked the passage to an understanding of the alter ego (1932: 111 et seq.).

These considerations permit the conclusion to consider as definitely refuted the idea that phenomenological sociology is the exclusive product of phenomenological thinking [21].

CHAPTER 4

THE RECEPTION OF BERGSON

In the third chapter, Ilja Srubar has shown in what way Schutz accepted ideas from Bergson and mobilized them for purposes of the development of his own conceptions of a multi-layered structure of self-experience, consciousness of self, experience and recognition of objects, and experience and recognition of "the Thou." As stated before, the Bergsonian basis of this undertaking consists of segments of the work of the French intuitionist and vitalist philosopher, selected for the purposes on hand. There is no need to either justify such a heuristic procedure or to offer reasons for not considering what, of Bergson's work as a whole, has been left out. Nevertheless, in this chapter, I will shift the focus of attention from Schutz's integration and transformation of Bergson's psychology of consciousness to Schutz's evaluation of Bergson during and beyond the period of 1924-1928. This appraisal will contain both positive and critical points; they will be pursued insofar as they can contribute to a better understanding of Schutz's acceptance of Bergsonian ideas into the permanent body of his own theories, and insofar as they can help clarify the reasons for which Schutz did not use Bergsonian psychology of consciousness uncritically but strove to go beyond it - as Srubar has aptly demonstrated in Chapter 3.

LASTING INFLUENCE OF BERGSON

In the outline drafts for the LIFE FORMS, Schutz provided for a chapter concerned with the appraisal of Bergson's philosophy, including a critical section. Positively, he spoke of the significance of Bergson's formulations for the problem of the founding of a theory of consciousness in Max Scheler's sense: Bergson's undertaking is "a first attempt at constructing ideal types of consciousness; a pointing-out of the inadequacy of the intellect to grasp the problem of duration; a dissolving of the polarity of the unity of the experiencing I and, through this, an overcoming of dualism of every kind, for instance: body - soul, spirit - matter, finalism - vitalism, causality - teleology, freedom of will - determinism" (1982: 18).

This attempt was based on Bergson's leading conceptions: duration as inner time in contrast to external (mundane and cosmic) time; memory as reflective activity in contrast to immediate experiencing of the Now and Thus; the conceptions of life and consciousness. In their ramifications, these ideas formed the core of the Bergsonian theories accepted by Schutz: pure and memory-endowed duration; the objectification of subjective states; symbolic representation and its effects; the transformations of qualitative experiences into quantitative interpretations and of the continuous flow of inner duration into discrete external space-time structures; the creation of meaning in a retrospective process; the simultaneity of living in inner duration and in the space-time world.

For Schutz, these and related conceptions were achievements which made Bergson into a figure of crucial significance in the development of Philosophy. Most of all, he praised him as "the first philosopher who forced modern Philosophy to accept this basic difference between experience in itself and reflection on experiences" (1982: 32) [1]. Henceforth, this differentiation should become a basic guideline for Schutz's dealing with phenomenological-psychological descriptions on the one hand, and phenomenological or sociological theories on the other. It did not merely guide Schutz in the project of 1924-1928; a few years later, it enlightened his analysis of the "constitution of the meaningful experience in its given duration": (1932: 43ff); in 1940-1941, it became a central point in his controversy with Talcott Parsons (1978), and it was repeatedly stressed in his later studies.

Aside from basic conceptions of Bergson, Schutz drew a good number of examples from his writings which illustrated them. Notably, they were taken from his ESSAI (TIME AND FREE WILL): observations of the movements of a pendulum of a clock; an algebraic notation of velocity; the apperception of the sounds of a clock striking the hour; the process of getting acquainted with a city into which one has recently moved; a diagram of the process of choosing; a diagram with algebraic notations illustrating the spatialization of time (E.T. of Bergson, 1889: 102-108, 117-119, 127, 129-130, 176, 191-192).

Beyond this, Bergson provided a number of specific ideas for Schutz which are so deeply embedded in his work as a whole that the discovery of their Bergsonian origin comes as a surprise. Among them are references to ready-made ideas, to common-sense thinking, and to the significance of the "life story" of the individual for his ongoing experiences in a given Here and Now. The last notion found its major expression in Schutz's conception of the "biographical situation" of the individual. Schutz's central interest in interactive and intersubjective constellations found support in Bergson's occasional elaboration of patterns of diadic interchange. Throughout his intellectual career, Schutz accepted and enhanced the age-old dialogical constellation of "Peter and Paul," a favorite example chosen by Bergson. On the same level of significance, but endowed with added methodological importance, lies Bergson's notion of the "conscious spectator" which appeared in Schutz's Bergson manuscripts as the "third person" (Bergson, E. T. 1889: 184ff, 108, 111).

The lasting significance of Bergson for Schutz found its full expression in the opening theme of DER SINNHAFTE AUFBAU DER SOZIALEN WELT. While this successful execution of the objective stated in the manuscripts of LIFE FORMS AND MEANING STRUCTURE was carried out after Schutz had greatly elongated his Bergsonian phenomenal-psychological baseline by the psycho-phenomenological base line of Husserl, he declared: "We take as point of departure for our further investigations the contrast, pointed out by Bergson, between simply living along in the stream of experience and life in the conceptual world of space and time" (1932: 43).

Schutz kept abreast with Bergson after the publication of his book. When, in 1934, he read the just published new essay collection of Bergson, LE PENSEE ET LE MOUVANT, he "felt happy to see that many important formulations of mine agree almost literally with Bergson's expositions - so, for instance, the thinking modo futuri exacti," thinking in the grammatical form which expresses a planned act or expected event as having been accomplished (letter to Fritz Machlup, 9/10/34).

In his American writings, Schutz's references to Bergson were not as frequent as in DER SINNHAFTE AUFBAU. Yet, they maintain the relevance of the French philosopher for his work, possibly second only to Husserl but with James coming close to it. This is not the place to broadly discuss the role Bergson continued to play in Schutz's work since 1940. Only a few highlights will be given. Largely, Schutz reconfirmed Bergson's contributions to sets of basic conceptions which had become standard ingredients of his own basic conceptions, on top of them again durée in its relations to immediate experiences and in connection with memory and other deliberate and cognitive activities. Particularly noteworthy, in this respect, may be his confirmation of "Bergson's statement that the real enigma involved in the phenomena of memory is not what we remember but what we forget" (1970: 15).

Further, and leading into broader spheres of Schutz's theoretical interests, we note his recognition of Bergson's view "that all our perceptions are determined by our activities" (1951a: 168 n. 2). Thereby, he accepted one pragmatic element in Bergson's thinking which could be integrated into a theory of volitional action. Most of all, he accepted Bergson's theory of free will and, in particular, his ingenious treatment of the problem of choice (for instance, 1951a: 175-177).

Schutz's lasting interest in the problem of relevance, a most crucial issue of his basic concerns, originated during his study of Bergson. The key to it was the French philosopher's conception of "attention to life," recognized by Schutz later as "the basic regulative principle of our conscious life" which, as "interest in life," does define "the realm of our world which is relevant to us" and even "determines the span and function of our memory" (1945c: 537). As "tension of our consciousness" (1970a: 96), it takes the form of attention to pragmatic actions in the sphere of the pursuits of interests in everyday life, but also makes for turning toward non-pragmatic spheres of experience and interest. Schutz's famous theory of multiple realities, released by his reading of James's considerations of "multiple universes," found its first inspiration in Bergson's conception of "attention to life." While Bergson himself preferred to treat the varieties of spheres of human experiences in bi-polar terms, Schutz considered as "one of the central points" of his philosophy an at least insipient "theory that our conscious life shows an indefinite number of different planes," ranging from that of action to that of dreams (1945c: 537).

This highly abbreviated characterization of the permanent effects of Bergsonian conceptions upon significant aspects of Schutz's life work makes clear that some of the important sections of the foundations of the latter bear the mark of their Bergsonian origin [2]. Together, these effective conceptions of Bergson form that segment of Bergson's philosophy which found acceptance by Schutz. It will now be possible to make some remarks about those parts of this philosophy which can be found on the far side of the line which we may imagine to have been drawn, by Schutz, across Bergson's body of thought.

EXCLUSION OF BERGSON'S EVOLUTIONISM

The introductory chapter on "Bergson's Intuitionist Philosophy" (1982: 12) was to start with a "presentation of the <u>not</u> biological part" of this philosophy. This, then constitutes a first clear cut across the ranges of Bergson's theories.

The statement about the exclusion of the biological part should not be misread. It does not extend to Bergson's treatment of the body as instrument, object, and in a sense subject of immediate experiences. On the contrary, Schutz followed Bergson's suggestions in this respect. In his early manuscripts as well as in later writings, he paid great attention to the close relationship between immediate experiences and bodily sensations. In the "first main part" of LIFE FORMS AND MEANING STRUCTURE (1982: 31-109), he dealt in considerable detail with the sensations issuing from the "body moved" passively and the actively "moving body" as a whole or in specific external parts of it. Thereby, he demonstrated almost painstakingly how somatic feelings of bodily movements enter into consciousness on the level of the life form of "memory-endowed duration" and transform themselves there into basic experiences of extension, of space traversed (see 1982, sections (12) - (14): 76-88). These considerations of the "somatic feeling of life" and the origin of the awareness of extension and space constitute a most relevant contribution of Schutz to the phenomenology of bodily experiences and of experiences not only mediated by but essentially issuing from Man's somatic life.

Their significance is the greater as they have been written at least fifteen years before Merleau-Ponty made his brilliant inquiries into the general areas of phenomenal and phenomenological psychology that was Schutz's concern from 1925 on. When Merleau-Ponty described his prime objective as that of re-establishing "the roots of the mind in its body and in its world" (1964: 3), he adequately described Schutz's objective as crystallized during the Bergson period of his work.

Schutz' exclusion of the "not biological part" of Bergson's philosophy from consideration concerned not the tenet of the somatic feeling of life but his biological-evolutionary theory. Thus, Bergson's first two studies (1889 and 1896) are hardly affected by it. Without doubt, however, it concerns Bergson's third book, L'évolution créatrice (1907). This study shows Bergson preoccupied with the "history of the evolution of life" and, in particular, with demonstrating "how the intellect has been formed, by an uninterrupted progress, along a line which ascends through the vertebrate series up to man" (E.T. 1944: xix). Of course, Bergson was not an evolutionist of the Darwinian and only in a limited sense of the Lamarckian kind. To assume the contrary means to assume that he completely negated not only everything he had set down in this early studies but also the principles he had reaffirmed, a few years before the publication of Creative Evolution in his "Introduction to Metaphysics" (1903). He did not bow to the rigidity of the "laws of evolution" postulated by the natural science evolutionists. His approach was aptly condensed by Irwin Edman, who wrote: "When ... Bergson turned to biological considerations, he held that change means growth, growth means creation, creation means freedom" (Foreword to 1944: xii). Yet, he nevertheless accepted the problem formulation of the original evolutionists and, thereby, engaged in imaginative yet speculative constructions which may have been plausible to many members of his own generation - even Williams James showed his interest by encouraging the translation of the book into English - but which Schutz, born forty years after Bergson, found not only devoid of theoretical usefulness for his work but objectionable in principle [3].

BEYOND BERGSON'S SCOPE

The second section of the planned Bergson chapter was called "Critique." However, it was not to contain critical argumentations against individual trains of thought and conceptions of Bergson, which Schutz found untenable. Since, on principle, he was not given to indulge in criticism for its own sake, he dealt here not with errors of commission but such of omission. The sub-topics he set down concerned missing explanations of problems which arose directly from tracts of Bergson's theoretical expositions.

Schutz wrote seven such sub-topics down in shorthand fashion. I will list them here, commenting on them as well as I can.

(a) "Extensives out of Intensives." Likely, this refers to the need for an explanation of the possibility of reaching an experiential and cognitive grasp of 'objects' and 'movements' in outer space from the originary grounds of inner duration which knows of no extension but is wholly "intensive."

(b) "Recognition of the inorganic in action (practical [?] line of the intellect)." This may refer to the need for an analysis of the experiential encounter of physical objects in the course of bodily action [4].

(c) "Solution of meaning." The intention of this point remains obscure to me. Possibly, Schutz aimed at the need for a satisfactory theory of "meaning" itself.

(d) "Where starts the function of the social?" This question refers to the need for establishing the point at which the quasi-solipsistic interpretations of the forms and processes of consciousness must take cognizance of intersubjective phenomena and pre-established means of communication, etc. (intersubjective relations, interaction, speaking and thinking in terms of a language).

(e) "Science problem and intuition." This point is best explained as a call for clarifying the relationship between the intuitions which flow from the spheres of immediate experiences and the typified and systematized knowledge which is embodied in conceptual thinking and finds its most consistent expression in scientific reasoning and its intellectual equipment. Philosophically speaking, this point aims at an epistemology which has room both for Bergson's intuition and Weber's rational cognition.

(f) " 'Unity of the I' and Social Person." This point hints at Schutz's conviction that an individual's self-perception is based on the feeling of the "unity of the I" in the face of the ever-changing quality experiences characteristic of the flow or duration. It makes the challenge of this unity thematic in the face of external social experiences, which, invariably, place the individual into partial roles and subject him to segmental typifications which, in turn become social self-typifications.

(g) "What is a symbol?" This, obviously, refers to the need for a clarification of the concept of 'symbol' within the framework of Bergson's philosophy and its extended application to some of its central themes.

Closely linked to these seven "critical" points are the five points which Schutz made in the third section of his plan for the Bergson chapter. The first designates omissions in Bergson's thinking, the second additions to it: desiderata. The title of this section is

"Requirements of a vitalist philosophy." Its initial phrase indicates that such a philosophy must have room for the treatment of the following sub-topics:

(h) "Thou and problem of meaning." This point suggests the reconsideration of the "problem of meaning" in the intersubjective context of social relationships. The next three points may be read as specifications of basic aspects of the problem of intersubjective meaning.

(i) "Understanding." This point seems to aim at one of the core aspects of what Schutz called the "Thou problem." It takes the existence of other beings "like me" for granted and aims at the exploration of the possibilities of "understanding" the other in terms of his motivations and interests within given interactional situations.

(j) "Typification." This points to a cognitive device which, often, serves as a short-cut to understanding others. According to Schutz's later theories, type notions are applied by anyone in given situations, according to pre-established ideas of 'typical' motives 'typical' interests and objectives, and 'typical' personality traits.

(k) "Symbol." This point is not clear to me. It is possible that Schutz wanted to refer to the "function" of symbols in intersubjective communication.

(l) "The social conditions, the mechanisms, and the technique of 'simultaneity' of living-in-space-and-time." This point, finally, seems to direct us to the nucleus of Schutz's theory of intersubjective understanding in the interactive spheres of what he eventually, with Husserl, came to call the life-world. The simultaneity alluded to may be that of the immediate experiences in inner duration of two individuals involved with one another within the same interactional situation, an event taking place in space and time of the outer world [5].

Whether considered omissions in, or additions to, Bergson's phenomenal-psychological considerations, these points give a good indication of Schutz's intention to move beyond the accepted body of Bergson's thought along a broad front which seems to contain all the important strategic objectives which were implied in the over-all plan for the study of 1924-1928. In other words, what had been announced innocuously as a short list of missing items, opened up into the whole program of Schutz's project of the Bergson period, which was as extensive as it was ambitious.

CRITIQUE OF BERGSON'S PHILOSOPHY

In the post-Bergsonian periods of his work, Schutz continued to refer rather frequently to Bergson. Occasionally, these positive references were interspersed with critical remarks. It would serve no purpose to repeat them here, with one exception. When, in 1942, he rejected Scheler's "data of a suprapersonal consciousness" as "metaphysical hypothesis," he found Bergson co-responsible (1942: 335) [6]. This, then, was one of his very occasional warnings not to mistake his acceptance of wide tracts of Bergson's thinking for an agreement with every metaphysical principle of the French philosopher.

It was only in the very last period of his life, when Schutz had become a full-time teacher and offered half of his courses in the Department of Philosophy at the New School, that he decided to face Bergson's philosophy as a whole.

In the Spring Term of 1958, he held a seminar on "William James and Henri Bergson" which he described, in the school catalogue, as a "study and discussion of selected writings of both philosophers with a view to an understanding of the interrelationship of their thought." There is evidence that he introduced two pieces of secondary literature - next to possible other ones - which contained extensive basic criticisms of Bergson: one by Santayana, the other by Horace Kallen [7].

Santayana's "Winds of Doctrine" had appeared in 1913; the book contained a chapter on Bergson: not a scholarly discussion but an in its way brilliant essayistic polemique against Bergson's evolutionary and vitalist doctrines. While Santayana praised the French thinker for his philosophical qualities and knowledge, he tore into him for what he called his lack of respect for the achievements of past philosophers; a result of his evolutionism according to which "later things" are necessarily better than earlier ones. On top of this, he ascribed to Bergson a historicism in a quasi-Hegelian sense. Both arguments, needless to say, issued from Santayana's conceptions of History and Tradition, as expressed in his monumental LIFE OF REASON. On the other hand, Santayana pitted his own brand of philosophical rationalism against the subjectivist intuitionism of Bergson, whom he characterized as being "instinctively a mystic" who is frightened of "non-human immensities" and "deliberately discredits the existence of anything except in immediacy" (1913: 82).

Santayana formulated Bergson's position as follows: "Things must be reduced again to what they seem; it is vain and terrible to take them for what we find they are." He is a victim of the "psychological illusion that our ideas and purposes are original facts and forces (instead of expressions in consciousness of facts and forces which are material) and the practical optical illusion that everything wheels about us in this world. Duration, by Bergson, is simply the "somewhat dazzling doctrine that to be is to last, or rather to feel oneself endure." While Bergson asserted that being is constantly in flux, in reality nothing happens in it: "To believe in real change you must put some trust in representation,and if you posit a real past and real future you posit independent objects. ... the flux becomes an idea of the absolute, like the image of a moving spiral, always flowing outwards or inwards, but with its centre and its circumference always immovable." Bergson is a "microscopic psychologist," studying "not some integrated passion or idea, but something far more recondite: the minute texture of sensation, memory, or impulse" (1913: 63, 72, 78, 98, 75).

Further, Santayana stressed that he was not adverse to biological vitalism as a natural force but that he had to reject Bergson's vital impetus as a "metaphysical force" which "breaks the continuity of nature." With this, Bergson was found to have refused "seeking to solve the only real problem, namely, how nature is actually constituted" (1914: 72-73, 93) [8].

Schutz did not reject the tradition of Western Rationalism as such; he granted Santayana a place in it (see 1952). He could understand but did not share that ontological realism which Santayana called materialistic. Likewise, he could understand but did not share the philosophy of history which he found in Santayana's work - in the same manner in which he could understand but did not share the philosophy of history of his friend, Eric Voegelin. But he had fended off the latter's attacks on Husserl's phenomenological psychology while granting his arguments against transcendental phenomenology. In the same manner, he could not have denied the justification of Santayana's attack on the metaphysical implications of Bergson's vitalism and evolutionism without thereby accepting the unrestrained attack on the principle of inner duration and on Bergson's phenomenal psychology of consciousness.

When Schutz placed Santayana's Bergson critique on the agenda of his seminar, he likely pursued two reasons. First, the chapter in question would serve, in a forceful manner, to refute the bad metaphysical notions in the body of Bergson's philosophy as a whole. Secondly, it would expose his students to likewise forceful arguments against Bergson's psychology of consciousness and, hopefully, induce them to find cogent counter-arguments in defense of it.

The thin volume by Horace Kallen, who was the most distinguished American-born thinker at the New School faculty [9], appeared one year after Santayana's "Winds of Doctrine." It was called WILLIAM JAMES AND HENRI BERGSON: A STUDY IN CONTRASTING THEORIES OF LIFE (1914). Kallen had been eminently qualified to write this comparison; he had been a personal student of James who entrusted him in his will with editing his last, unfinished, manuscript on "Some Problems of Philosophy." During a longer sojourn in Europe, likely at the suggestion of James, he also studied with Bergson [10].

Kallen identified with James's pragmatism, which he described as an antidote against metaphysics and monistic systems of world interpretation. He presented the "pragmatic method" as a way of establishing the meaning of propositions by their practical consequences: James' philosophy is radical empiricism. It interprets the world as an "infinite of orders" which, in turn, can be approached from all possible angles.

Measuring Bergson's metaphysics on this pragmatism, Kallen found it unacceptable. In his critical task, he based himself essentially on two publications of Bergson which appeared in the first decade of the Twentieth Century: "Introduction of Metaphysics" (1903) and CREATIVE EVOLUTION (1907). Only rarely did he refer to the 'psychological' studies of 1889 and 1896. When he cited them, so for the purpose of singling out individual passages which seem to contain the roots of Bergson's later metaphysical speculations. Bergson's thing, Kallen argued, betrayed three fallacious characteristics inherent in the "philosophical tradition": Love of wholeness inducing system building, assumption of universal primordinal "elements" which count as "reality" in the metaphysical system, and assigning a "compensatory nature" to reality which makes it homogeneous with human nature and human values.

Reasoning back from Bergson's later metaphysical constructions to his earlier work, Kallen did no longer accept the original expositions of inner duration and memory as phenomenal descriptions. Instead, he insisted that, by Bergson, "ultimate reality is of the same stuff as our inner life." Intuition, he added, therefore is no longer a means of "getting at" spontaneous processes of consciousness; by Bergson it has become a method which reveals "fundamental reality in the traditional metaphysical sense." It has become a tool of metaphysical speculation which ends up with the postulation of an extrinsic 'Creator-God" (1914: 105, 127, 105-106, 125, 126).

Since James had shown a great positive interest in Bergson's work, Kallen conceded that his teacher had been attracted by the former's "treatment of concepts in their relation to activity, movement, and life." He gained from Bergson "freedom to accept experience at its face value" which is "not illusory" (1914: 147). While this is no small compliment for Bergson, Kallen argued that James put these fundamental insights to a philosophical use which was the opposite of Bergson's. Although not couched in such terms, his criticism lends itself to the following reformation: After a seemingly radical beginning in Husserl's sense, which did not bring a total separation of his thinking from traditional metaphysical notions, Bergson succumbed to the temptation of creating a comprehensive philosophical "system" of his own and, thereby fell into 'bad' metaphysical speculation.

It is of interest to note that Schutz valued Kallen's attack on Bergson highly because he was "amazed to see to what extent the author anticipated the later development of Bergson's ideas ... " (Letter to University of Chicago Press of 1/17/58). Kallen had developed a basic criticism not only of the then published sections of Bergson's philosophy, which had remained on the far side of his earlier phenomenal psychology of consciousness; he had already seen the further consequences of the development of Bergson's philosophy after 1915.

When offering the seminar of 1958, Schutz may have felt that he owed it to his students to provide them with an adequate critique of the grandiose evolutionary theories which, so far, he had merely ignored. In this, he may have been re-enforced by additional considerations. Since the mid-Fifties, he had been involved in a quite thorough criticism of Husserl's transcendental phenomenology and eventually also of parts of his eidetic theories. Critically transgressing the boundary lines of phenomenological psychology, which he had originally drawn for his phenomenological work, he may have felt the necessity to take a similar step with regard to the other fundamental figure in his philosophical thought. Kallen had done this long before him from the perspective of James' pragmatism. He did not have to accept the latter in justification of Kallen's Bergson critique. He could make it vicariously his own.

Both Santayana and Kallen aimed at the total rejection of Bergson's philosophy. For Schutz, the reason for accepting their criticism was in a way the opposite: He supported the sharp attacks on the untenable theories and speculations of Bergson's in order to better protect his pertinent psychology of consciousness from all-out attacks and to better preserve it as a most relevant contribution to the understanding of the subjectivity of human experience [11].

CHAPTER 5

WEBER'S METHODOLOGY AND BERGSON'S PSYCHOLOGY: BASIC TENSIONS WITHIN A DUALISTIC PROJECT

The years between 1924 and 1928 present themselves as a transitional period in the scholarly life of Schutz. Of course, he did pursue the project of these years as a definite undertaking. His objective was to find a secure foundation for Weber's sociology of understanding; he was convinced that he would gain it from Bergson's writings. And, indeed, these writings offered him a wealth of insights and suggestions and inspired him to develop wide ranges of a phenomenal psychology of consciousness. Yet, toward the end of his Bergsonian period, Schutz had to realize that he was at an impasse: the project could not be finished with the means offered by Bergson or developed from a baseline constructed with their help.

Yet, as indicated both in Chapters 3 and 4, Bergson provided Schutz with an array of theoretical equipment which should become part of the permanent stock of his life work. He even provided him with the impulse to move beyond him in the direction of objectives he had set for himself before studying Bergson's psychology of consciousness; however, it was not strong enough to carry him to his destination.

This chapter will focus on one general characteristic of this transitional study: the dualism rooted in Schutz's use of Weber's methodology for constructing the theory of the life forms and his mobilization of data for substantive evidence which had been gained by way of introspection in the manner of Bergson.

The combination worked surprisingly well - up to certain limits. Beyond them, it gave rise to difficulties which, in my opinion, decided the fate of the whole project.

FROM EPISTEMOLOGY TO ONTOLOGY

In their entirety, the manuscripts of Schutz's Bergson period show him on his way from the philosophical, social-scientific, and psychological orientations he had acquired during his study years and both consolidated and amended during the first three or four years of his professional life; they led him to the orientations which he offered for public scrutiny in 1932.

Philosophically, he had emerged from his academic training period as a "believer in neoKantian philosophy," as he wrote to Natanson. Entering the realm of Bergson's philosophical reasoning, he abandoned this base line, which was practically obligatory for the Central-European students of his generation. He now found that the philosophy of the last fifty years - which in Central Europe was dominated by the neoKantian schools - had nothing accomplished which would be of help to the GEISTESWISSENSCHAFTEN (1982: 15).

Nevertheless, he found it necessary to face up to Kant himself [1]. In his outline for the project of 1924-1928, he provided for three lanes of access to the central problems of his undertaking, characterized by the names of Kant, Weber, and Bergson. Thus, he provided for an "Attempt at Gaining Access by Way of Kant and the Apriori-Theory." The problem to be illuminated thereby was that of founding (Fundierungsproblem) - a term Schutz had taken over from Max Scheler who, in turn, had accepted it from Husserl; it refers to the original ground from which philosophizing has to start and which could not be reduced to something else [2].

In one of the drafts of an introduction for his planned book, Schutz dealt in some detail with Kant's answer to the "problem of founding" (1982: 19-20). He found Kant's solution lacking on account of his operating on merely "one plane," that of the "logical-cognitive formation of concepts." By limiting metaphysics to epistemology and to the question, "How are synthetical judgments a priori possible," and by confining religion to the sphere of pure reason, he demonstrated "the limits of the intellectualization of these realms but not the boundaries of the realms themselves." Yet, both "are open to experience on the far side of these limitations." His "epistemological formalism" led him to deal with "all essential questions of life ... merely as antinomies or contradictions." Even Kant's "moral imperative in me," the foundation of his tenet of "the primacy of practical reason, merely show the renunciation, by the intellect, of the foray into the realm of life."

Schutz concluded that the whole transcendental logic of Kant "is tailor-made for cognition" and, by definition, cut out merely "a well-defined sector from reality" according to principles "which are postulated a priori as ultimate logical necessities" (Denknotwendigkeiten).

While rather rudimentary, these considerations show how Schutz came to terms with Kant. He did not declare him obsolete. Rather, he indicated that his epistemology was confined to that "well-defined sector of reality" which represents the realm of ratiocination or, in

Schutz's terms of 1925, the life form of the thinking I. This, in principle, amounted to a recognition of Kant's immense contribution within its properly delineated confines without, of course, foregoing the privilege of its critical appraisal [3]. Schutz's crucial conclusion was that Kant had not dealt with the broad array of other realms of human experience and, more, that his system had no room for their interpretation. It follows, then, that Kantian philosophy did not offer Schutz an access to the problem which he had posed with the plan for his studies of 1924-1928.

We may call this the 'methodological' insufficiency of Kant's thinking for Schutz's purposes. Philosophically, he had stated that Kant's restriction of metaphysics to epistemology makes inaccessible "deeper areas" not yet described as ontologically recognizable. It stands to reason, then, that Schutz had in mind to move from Kantian epistemology to an as yet undefined kind of ontology. Immediately, Bergson comes to mind as a likely source of an ontological orientation appropriate to the understanding and interpretation of experiences "on the far side" of Kant's rationalist limitations. But, while Bergson's early work was farthest on the far side of Kant, it did not contain an adequate ontology. "The 'Introduction to Metaphysics' (1903), a remarkable document of Bergson's philosophy of intuition, amounts actually to a masterly recounting of his psychology of consciousness and its defense against incompatible philosophical approaches, such as traditional empiricism or rationalism, Kant included. The essay contains one basic ontological statement: "There is an external reality which is given immediately to our mind" [4]. But this proposition, propped up by a few interpretative paragraphs, is at best the nucleus of an ontology which Bergson failed to develop. Instead, he concentrated on explaining that "metaphysics is to proceed by intuition," thus stressing the way by which metaphysical insights are to be gained., Thereby, he replaced ontology by a basic philosophical methodology which, in turn, is undistinguishable of the methodology of his psychology of consciousness.

Schutz cut himself off from Kantian epistemology. This step did not and could not enable him to reach an adequate ontological anchor ground within the confines of Bergson's philosophy. On the contrary, he discovered that Bergson, in the work of his middle period, had selected "a biological natural-science orientation as path into metaphysics" (1982: 18). The movement away from Kantianism left him floating in a direction indicated by Bergson's early philosophy without, however, bringing the more reliable shores of a different metaphysics into sight.

During the years of the intensive study of Husserl, which followed his Bergson period, Schutz became a phenomenologist. The absorption and integration of Husserl's phenomenological psychology and of his phenomenological method pushed the ontological problem temporarily into the background [5] or, rather, postponed its discussion. In a concluding section of his first book, Schutz was "pointing out further problems." He mentioned "three clusters" of them, one of which concerned the "constitution of the Thou as such." He expected that the solution of this problem would simultaneously bring "the solution of the problem of the intersubjective validity of our experience of the world as such." In this context, he mentioned Husserl's recent announcement of a new investigation which would put this question into the center. But, he added, its "definite solution may only be gained from an ontology of man built upon a phenomenological basis" (1932: 285). Thereby Schutz designated the target of a 'phenomenological' ontology still to be created. Later, he identified such an ontology essentially as a philosophical anthropology; it would be identical with an ontology of the life-world. He realized that, with this objective he went counter to Husserl's conviction that a general ontology is unnecessary for his philosophy. For Schutz it was needed but unattainable by the "rigorous scientific method" of phenomenology; and he was not afraid to face the consequences: "There exist fundamental philosophical problems," he wrote to his friend, Eric Voegelin, in 1943, "which demand the courage to enter metaphysics" (11/11/43).

While one can find numerous hints and short statements about these ontological-anthropological problems scattered over Schutz's American writings and his correspondence with various scholars, he did hardly more than keeping this task on the agenda. Being his possibly most significant philosophical project, it should remain unexecuted.

DEALING WITH THE BERGSONIAN PARADOX

The central substantive concern of, and the primary intellectual motive for, Schutz's early project was to give Weber's sociology of understanding an adequate subjective psychological-philosophical underpinning: to carry out its 'founding' in the phenomenological sense. With some reservations, he chose Bergson's "attempt at a solution" as the baseline of this planned undertaking.

Now, the most characteristic means of Bergson's phenomenal-psychological investigations was intuition - or, in the term Husserl adopted later, meditation. But Bergson gave no account of this 'method,' and this understandably so: It was not a technique of disciplined observation, in which one may be trained as in the use of a microscope. Rather, it was the gift of inner sensitivity turned into self-observation. The gift cannot be acquired but, if it is given to a thinker, he can sharpen, direct, and in a sense control its application to his own consciousness. Bergson had it and made use of it, taking its existence for granted. As demonstrated most of all in the manuscript of the first main part of the project of 1924-1928, Schutz too had this gift; and he too took it for granted. The 'method' of intuitive self-contemplation was made problematic neither by Bergson nor by Schutz.

Schutz made a crucial 'methodological' step when he began to execute his plan of giving Weber's sociology of understanding its proper phenomenal-psychological foundation. Through Weber, he anchored himself firmly in the realm of rigorous conceptual thinking and the construction of theoretical models and types. Through Bergson, he penetrated into the realm of intuitive contemplation and phenomenal-descriptive procedures. Forthwith, he should operate on both levels, remaining conscious of their differences and preventing a careless intermingling both of substantive findings and 'methodological' procedures characteristic of either realm.

One may conclude that Schutz reserved the first of these levels for sociology and the second for phenomenal psychology. This would not be false but does not hit the core of the differentiation: Conceptual reasoning is not confined to social-science matters, it pertains also to introspective data. Schutz wrote: "The method of a science of experience can only consist of acts of self-inspection." However, he felt that not much more could be done beyond stating this tenet. Thus, he immediately continued that "a book must needs language" and "is forced to resort to conceptual formulations." It would be foolish trying "to break through the cover of language and concept." The best one can hope for is "irradiate this cover" and get the shadow image of a vague outline of what is below it (1982: 70). To speak about it means to resort to symbols, not in the least the symbols of a conceptual language.

This did not erase the difference between the two spheres. Yet, there was "no reason to be afraid of the spectre of the syncretism of methods," that is, the mixing of seemingly contradictory methodological procedures, "which is feared in every theoretical and empirical discipline" (1982: 70). This point may have been well taken. But Schutz made it without offering further explanations, although it seems that they were urgently called for. He obviously had decided that there was no more to be said about intuition and introspection, and concentrated on methodological considerations which fell within the realm of conceptual reasoning and, in specific, concept construction.

It was only when he encountered Husserl's intriguing expositions of phenomenal-intuitive meditations that he recognized that, even with the inadequate means of linguistic description, more could be done than he had been prepared to admit under the sway of Bergson. Most of all, Husserl convinced him of the potential fruitfulness of the "phenomenological method" which is quite articulated yet stands in sharp contrast to any method developed in the fields of the social sciences.

In any case, within the ranges of the Bergsonian project, Schutz fastened his methodological attention as good as exclusively on what, loosely, is the form of Bergson's early expositions. The French thinker's problem formulation, he stated, "is a first attempt at constructing ideal types of consciousness" (1982: 18). The question as to where the "material" - to fall back upon an expression he liked to use at the time - for the construction of these ideal types came from, will have occurred to Schutz, but he did not set it down. It may well be that he was so overwhelmed by the immediate 'evidence' of Bergson's insights - as occurring to his own intuitive glance - that the formulation of this problem itself seemed redundant. Setting down the accounts of the results of intuitive observations was all that seemed necessary. By contrast, he felt the need to spell out what the theoretical formulation of Bergson's investigative exploits represents methodologically.

The reason for this was what I have called the Bergson paradox, a paradox of which Bergson was fully aware. After a reiteration of his conception of pure duration, he remarked: "... by the very language I was compelled to use, I betrayed a deeply ingrained habit of setting out time in space. From this spatial setting-out, already accomplished, we are compelled to borrow the terms which we use to describe the state of a mind which has not yet accomplished it: these terms are thus misleading from the very beginning, and the idea of a multiplicity without relation to number or space, although clear for pure reflective thought, cannot be translated into the language of common sense" (1889: 124).

Clearly, this means that the experiences of and in inner duration are utterly unsuitable for expression and description in everyday language. Language sprang up from pragmatic necessities; it is best adapted to the description of external objects distributed in space and their occurrence in discrete 'moments' of time which itself is 'spatialized' contrary to its continuous and nontangible character. Schutz, of course, was well aware of the paradox issuing from the attempt to force into linguistic forms and freeze into rigid words what is ever flowing experience of pure and ever unrepeatable qualities. But he seemed not to be worried about it. On the contrary, he was sure that the paradox was "merely apparent." It would disappear during the careful investigation of "the mechanics of the process by which our memory transforms the streaming and becoming of merely continual qualities into the concepts of extension and matter." There were two reasons for remaining confident that this transition could be made without falling either into the trap of Berkeley's solipsistic subjectivism or that of a metaphysical credo, like Leibniz's idea of a "pre-established harmony." First of all, memory itself "partakes in our inner duration": it bridges the chasm between immediate experience and the external space-time world. Secondly, the "moving body," as executive organ of the "acting I," initiates immediate experiences which occur in inner duration. The somatic feeling of body movements directly conveys a sensation of space. It bridges the gap between an elementary self-experience in inner duration and the extensiveness of external space [6]. Like memory, bodily movement belongs to both worlds.

These considerations do not answer the question which could be posed by adherents of a traditional (that is, Kantian) epistemology: "How does the extended object enter into my unextended apperception?" Schutz pointed out that Bergson ignored this problem and that he himself did "not pretend to solve the epistemological problem" as such. Rather, his formulation indicated a more limited objective: "Which path did the (memory, HRW) image traverse from our duration to the concept?" Attention, then, was shifted from epistemological concerns to the description of what Schutz had called "the mechanics of the process" of the transformation of experiences into conceptual ideas (1982: 42).

With this shift, Schutz believed to have found a way to avoid difficult problems both of epistemological or ontological and of empirical-psychological nature. Having come to Bergson's philosophy by way of Weber's sociology, he had no difficulties either in re-interpreting the idea of pure duration as an ideal-typical construct or in accepting the methodological consequences of this decision. Resolutely, he introduced his brand of ideal-typical methodology at the outset of his undertaking, making it into the over-all means of the construction of the whole theory of the life forms. It was to allow the "arbitrary construction of ideal types of the facts of consciousness which are experienced undifferentiated and as a whole in the totality of life." These arbitrary constructions, again, were to be subjected to "artificial analysis." The whole procedure was "exclusively justified by its purposiveness, its output of results" (1982: 17).

Thereby, the life forms became heuristic devices which, by definition, were not in need of epistemological or ontological justification. In its surprising simplicity, this decision eliminated the Bergson paradox with one stroke of the pen. As shown in earlier chapters, Schutz achieved quite respectable results on this basis. It worked, as any heuristic procedure, as long as the ideal-typical set-up was adequate to the problem it was supposed to solve. The only question was whether Schutz would be able to stay within this limited problem range or whether inherent necessities of his topic, consciousness, or else his original presuppositions in approaching it made it unavoidable to face additional problems - problems beyond heuristic expedience. This remains to be seen.

In any case, at the time Schutz was convinced that the ideal-typical method, which Weber had used - with convincing success - in his large-scale socio-historical investigations, could be used equally successfully in quite different areas of the human sciences. I am tempted to say that, within the specific setting of the project on the LIFE FORMS, Schutz expected from Bergson's work help in solving problems posed but not answered by Weber, and he saw in Weber's ideal-typical method the means to harness Bergson's psychology for his initial theoretical purposes.

PURE DURATION: A PROBLEM

This particular Weber-Bergson-Weber circularity is a basic feature of the design of the project of the LIFE FORMS. In the second part of the present study, I will be concerned with a number of consequences and implications of this design pattern as well as with various topical areas in which Schutz, whether inadvertently or intentionally, broke through the circle.

Nevertheless, I will here and now take up the discussion of the crucial conception of Bergson's psychology of consciousness, that of duration (durée), or rather of the place Schutz assigned to it in his ideal-typical scheme of the life forms and the difficulties which arose from this integration. It may seem that, thereby, I am running ahead of myself. But I hope that it will become clear in the course of the unfolding of my argument that the discussion of the basic concept of duration is needed here as introduction to, and preparation for, the critical appraisal of Schutz's first project which pays attention to more specific topics in selected aspects and details.

In the second chapter of this book, Ilja Srubar has given a good characterization of Bergson's notion of duration in its phenomenal-psychological connotations. In the third chapter he showed basic aspects of its integration into Schutz's project. Being fortunate enough to be able to rely on these expositions, I can take the matter from here.

It will be helpful to begin with pointing out that duration appears in Bergson's writings in two forms: durée and durée pure. When Schutz translated these two terms into German, he was aware that the German term, Dauer (duration) has about the opposite connotation from Bergson's term, durée. Like the English term, duration, its German equivalent stands for persistence over (a long) time; it is one of the non-specific notions of external time which Bergson had in mind when he spoke about "laying out time in space" [7]. Therefore, Schutz had to qualify both terms by an adverb, speaking of innere Dauer and reine Dauer, and in his American period of inner duration and pure duration.

There is a significant difference between the two terms. Inner duration denotes experiences in the flow of consciousness. As long as they are going on, they go on spontaneously and thus, as Schutz said, they are meaning-less, i.e., free of meaning. However, they are recognizable in retrospection after having-passed-away. As passed spontaneous experiences, they become cognizable; they can be interpreted retrospectively and endowed with meanings. However, at least according to Schutz's investigations of memory in LIFE FORMS, what we grasp in retrospective glance, is not the experience itself but its first memory image. Or, maybe, we could better say that just having-passed-away experience turns into such a first memory image in the very act of retrospection. This follows necessarily from the fact that any act of interpretation and of giving-meaning-to-something is an act of cognition. This leads to the recognition of the unavoidability of Bergson's paradox. Re-cognition, in this context, is translation of experience into cognition, and that means essentially into some terms of ordinary language. In this form, the paradox is not only unavoidable but also acceptable. When we clarify introspective 'data' cognitively for ourselves and/or convey them to others, we do the humanly best we can within the irrevocable conditions and limitations of our human existence.

Seen exclusively from this angle, there seems to exist no pertinent reason why the description of memory images of experiences in inner duration should not be subjected to further methodological treatment, such as applied by Schutz when he typified such data by placing them under classificatory categories, called life forms, and subjected the latter to further treatment by setting them up as ideal types. If this procedure could be considered objectionable, so for additional reasons. However, for the purposes of the present argument, I am not interested in finding out whether such reasons can be found or not.

If Schutz had solely been concerned with experiences in inner duration and their methodological-theoretical treatment, nothing more would have to be said. But, this was not the case.

Bergson had linked his considerations of experiences in inner duration to his term, pure duration. To my understanding, his formulations, in this respect are not too clear. Yet, since he used two different terms, it stands to reason that he had in mind a difference in their connotation. He offered quite similar characterizations - almost vivid descriptions - of both durée and durée pure (inner and pure duration) yet, at least implicitly seemed to aim the first expression at concrete experiences, and the second at the general connotation of the term; that is, duration in the abstract. Schutz decided to bring the difference out into the open. He wrote: "It is impossible immediately to experience pure duration, even by intuition." Thus, it cannot be translated into the 'empirically-descriptive' terms of a pheno-psychologist. Consequently, he called it "an unexecutable hypostasis," meaning here a theoretical construction which forthwith is treated as if it presented a fundamental reality. But, since Schutz wanted to use the concept nevertheless, he backed up somewhat by re-categorizing pure duration as a "necessarily marginal concept (Grenzbegriff), an unexecutable postulate" (1983: 22-23). Hypostatization is an unexusable scholarly fallacy; a marginal concept is a scientifically accepted methodological device. Schutz, thereby, could make pure duration into his first and lowest life form. He explained that Bergson did the only possible thing when he started with a "symbol-penetrated" life form, that of memory-endowed duration: By definition, pure duration is "memory-less"; "the last stratum to which we can penetrate is already 'memory-endowed'," and "pure duration can only be deduced with the help of the symbol system of the more complex life form" (1982: 23). But, since it "can be deduced," he did not hesitate to make it into the foundation of his system of life forms.

Seen epistemologically, "pure duration" seems to be a parallel case to Kant's "thing as such." But while Kant used his insight into the impossibility of asserting anything about the "thing" outside of its appearance in human perception in order to deal a heavy blow to the traditional scholastic Realism which had remained unchallenged up to his days, Bergson - and Schutz following him - had use for "pure duration" which would be "inner duration" without its experienced content.

One may be inclined to accept the construct of pure duration as a "pure" deduction from the observations underlying "inner duration" in its "memory-endowed" forms. One may agree that it is a logical necessity or marginal concept, a fictional zero-point, or a kind of first principle for rounding out an otherwise consistent theoretical system referring to observable complexes of data. But I find it difficult to agree that it can be considered an ideal type, the term taken in Weber's sense. To be a construct - a term which may fit any abstract concept - is not enough to call it an ideal type, even though any such type is a construct. To fill Weber's criteria, in general accepted by Schutz without reservation, the construct must be compatible with concrete empirical evidence. Schutz, however, made clear that - in contrast to all other life forms introduced by him - this criterion is not fulfilled. He himself stated that he did "not intend to assert the impossibility of pure duration without memory ... but only the impossibility of experiencing it immediately in the sense of 'evidence." He defined evidence "as 'Being-Thus' experience of a 'Now and Thus' " (1982: 23). Well: no evidence (tangible data) means no compatibility with empirical 'realities,' and that means no ideal type.

Shifting my attention from methodological-sociological to phenomeno-logical-psychological considerations, I will venture the following opinion: Maybe the whole issue is similar to that of the case of intentionality: The term is meaningless without reference to an intended object; it is always intentionality of something; to speak of "pure" intentionality does not make sense. Should we not also conclude that we never experience duration as such, but only duration of 'something,' of any kind of experience which can be grasped in retrospection and that speaking of "pure" duration is non-sensical?

TRANSITIONAL REMARK

In this chapter, I have tried to present the general framework, and in a way, set the tone for the second part of this study. In it, I will offer a hopefully balanced picture of both the positive aspects and results of Schutz's project of the LIFE FORMS and its negative aspects, its shortcomings and inherent contradictions within specific topical areas.

PART II

AN APPRAISAL

FAILURES AND LASTING CONTRIBUTIONS

One cannot do justice to Schutz's Bergson manuscripts by considering them to be of mere biographical-historical interest. Without them, he would not have been able to write his pioneering work, DER SINNHAFTE AUFBAU DER SOZALEN WELT, a book published five years after he had suspended his earlier project. The latter was not a 'negative experience' which, eventually, made him chose a viable path to the pursuit of his original target. It left him with a considerable amount of notions and insights which were indispensable for the whole conception underlying his first major publication. The intense occupation with Bergson had readied him for the acceptance of the phenomenological approach: "Prepared by my study of Bergson's philosophy, I found immediately Husserl's thought and language understandable" (1977: 42), when he encountered them in THE PHENOMENOLOGY OF INTERNAL TIME-CONSCIOUSNESS.

A part of Bergson's phenomenal psychology entered into DER SINNHAFTE AUFBAU and, through it, into the whole life work of Schutz. For this reason, the manuscripts of 1924-1928 demand the same careful attention as any other major piece of his writings. This attention will have to be critical, the term used in the original sense of the expression, critique: the art of scrutinizing and appraising any object of serious consideration. The main purpose of such critique, here, is the elucidation of implied or stated meanings, of unsuspected implications, and the general inspection of basic presuppositions on the one hand, and of cognitive consequences on the other. The discovery of fallacious reasoning or of errors of thinking may result from the pursuit of this objective; it is not its main target.

To approach Schutz's Bergson manuscripts in this sense means to take them scholarly serious and to treat them as relevant for the current issues and problems which have been posed in his work as a whole or which have been derived from it. In this sense, the Bergson manuscripts of Schutz are philosophically as alive as any other of his contributions.

PROGRAM FOR THIS PART

Like the first part, the second part consists of five chapters. In them I will treat some of the relevant issues Schutz touched upon in the Bergson manuscript, all of which have not been adequately treated (Chapter 6); expose his possibly most important contribution, the conception of the "somatic feeling of life" (Chapter 7); indicate the strains in the manuscripts introduced by the use of an ideal-typical framework and the decision to place the concrete, mundane ego into the center of the psychology of consciousness (Chapter 8); point out the touches of phenomenology, in the sense of Husserl's Ideas I, which appear in the manuscripts of 1924-1928 (Chapter 9); and finally discuss the possible reasons for Schutz to abandon the project after long years of intense efforts (Chapter 10).

BEYOND SCHUTZ?

The execution of this appraisal program will result in the presentation of implications, the continuation of trains of thought broken off at some point, the anticipation of answers to problems posed but not answered by Schutz, and the treatment of problems not posed but emerging from positions he developed. Needless to say, this is a somewhat precarious undertaking for which I have to assume full responsibility.

I can claim reasonable certainty only for Schutz's passages and statements, 'as far as they go,' which are my points of departure for further conclusions of whatever kind. Insofar as I am offering 'extrapolations' of trends in Schutz's thinking during his Bergson years, I feel to be on relatively safe grounds as long as I have been able to point out ideas he spelled out in his book of 1932 and which can be judged as 'points of destination' of the earlier trends. I grant that, in some case, this may be a matter of judgment with which other informed phenomenologists may differ. This is the risk I have to take; I think that any serious author involved in the interpretation of the work of others has to face this risk. Finally, I have drawn lines which transcend Schutz's positions as ascertainable in his later work.

Some readers of the present study may feel that I should have pointed out these occasions: I should neither give the impression that I make Schutz responsible for my own thoughts nor put my candle under the pail - to use a biblical expression. This may all be well and good; but even with the best intentions I could not do, within the confines of the present study, what would be desirable to do. First of all, in the last nine years I have worked so closely with the literary heritage of Schutz in its totality that I cannot always be sure where his thinking stopped and my continuations began. It would take some tedious re-investigations in order to ascertain this. By the same token, I fear, it would take tedious expositions to make distinctions of this kind in every possible case. Therefore, the readers in question will have to accept instead this my general admission of having transcended Schutz at various occasions [1].

It is my intention to make the second part of this limited study a modest contribution to one strand of the phenomenological approach. In the light of this goal, it is a secondary flaw if, in one or the other case, a reader is unable to place blame - or praise - on the doorsteps of Schutz or me, one of his students. I am convinced that this flaw will have little bearing on the success or failure of my attempt to bring to attention potential contributions to the present-day practice of some types of phenomenological work which originated in Schutz's first major albeit unfinished project.

CHAPTER 6

RELEVANT ISSUES - INADEQUATE EXECUTION

In this chapter, I will refer to a few technical points which concern sundry parts of the manuscripts. Most of all, however, I will critically inspect a small number of topics ("problems"), which are highly important for the subsequent work of Schutz but whose treatment in the present group of manuscripts, in comparison with their development in later writings, appears to be inadequate. The theoretical intention expressed in them is relevant, their execution unsatisfactory. This is due to two reasons. First, Schutz was not yet in command of an adequate conceptual-theoretical equipment for dealing with them; secondly, he broke off their exploration prematurely [1]. The critique contained in this chapter, then, is critical in the sense of an effort to preserve the theoretical intention by freeing it from the inadequate form in which it found its first expression.

Aside from the more technical items, four points will be discussed: Schutz's technique of representation, insofar as it consisted of diagrams and algebraic formulations; the notion of memory images; his dealing with the concepts of function and symbol in their application to his theorem of symbol function; and his adaptations of the subject-object dichotomy.

These themes seem to present partial issues which are independent of one another. However, their treatment will indicate that they are connected in the sense that they are symptoms of strains which inhere in the over-all conceptions of the theory of the life forms. Thus, they lead up to the general issue of the relationship between the over-all structure of his theory and the theoretical-philosophical-psychological purposes it was meant to serve. This will be taken up in the next chapters. - Speaking generally, the first two points show the marks of Bergson's thinking, both positively and negatively; the third invokes standard equipment of European academic reasoning; and the fourth seems to display lingering influences of neoKantian conceptions

Characteristic for all these points is that Schutz did not consistently maintain the basic position he had circumscribed for his investigations. Pursuing these issues, he came invariably upon insights which were at variance with these interpretations and indicated the points at which the shells of his own positions could be pierced.

These insights were gained by introspection and pointed - in various degrees of distinctiveness - toward a phenomenological understanding of the themes which had been developed within an 'artificially' constructed conceptual framework.

INTENT AND TERMINOLOGY

In the intellectual life story of Schutz, the Bergson manuscripts are documentations of his transition from traditional academic orientations, accepted in his student years or his early post-doctoral period, to phenomenological orientations. In a subtle manner, this transition manifested itself also in matters of terminology and formulation.

In the "Editor's Introduction" to Schutz's LIFE FORMS AND MEANING STRUCTURE, I have drawn attention to some of the terminological features of these manuscripts (1982: 7-9). Although written from a translator's point of view, these "Notes on Terminology" are relevant for present purposes. Should the reader be interested, he may resort to these pages. I will confine myself here to a few comments.

His speaking of "materials" when referring to data of observations would not merit mentioning were it not for his declaration of having been "forced to deal mainly with 'pre-scientific materials.'" This was so because the subject matter of the sociology of understanding is rooted in the "Thou problem," which "certainly is situated in the pre-scientific sphere" (1982: 70). The expression, then, stood for a crucial target of his investigations.

There seems to be a striking discrepancy between the use of this term - and of some others as well - and the stated intention. But, instead dwelling on such flaws, I shall stress the tremendous significance of the intention which Schutz expressed in a terminologically inadequate form. He formulated the same intention and gave it a clear direction also in other parts of his project. Thus, in one draft of his introduction, he spoke of "expected maximal results of the investigation," among them a "demonstration of the identity of duration and Thou as exclusive primary facts of consciousness" and a procedure leading "from life to thinking" (1982: 17). These programmatical points alone show that, already at the onset of the Bergson period, he was fully aware of the primacy of the spheres of experience and everyday life.

That means, he already saw that this sphere, later called the life-world, is the originary ground of other spheres of experience and activity. To call it "pre-scientific" means to stand the actually pertaining relationship between life-world and sciences on its head. Science, as a highly artificial and extremely 'rationalized' sphere of reasoning and interpretative activities, is 'post-life-worldly,' if it is permitted to coin such an expression.

At some points, Schutz's intentions were ahead of his terms. At one or the other occasion, however, he seemed to come up with terms adequate to his intentions; so, when he spoke of "phenomenon" or "phenomena." Yet, a note of caution may be in order. The terms were common in the Central-European academic language of the time. The 'subjective' connotations they had been given by the early proponents of phenomenology were widely unknown. I strongly suspect that Schutz used them in the older sense. This goes particularly for his speaking of the "phenomenon of memory." The grammatical singular alone points either to the abstract category of memory or - more likely in view of Schutz's acquaintance with Bergson's theory of memory which I would not call a phenomenological theory in Husserl's sense - an abstract "mental capacity." [2]

Other issues of terminology and expression could be mentioned [3], but most all of them would be even more occasional than those mentioned. However, there is one exception: Schutz's deliberate and persistent use of one type of technical device for mere illustrative and thus auxiliary purposes. Its discussion will precede that of the announced inspection of a few topics of importance for Schutz's later work but treated inadequately in his first project.

ATOMISTIC ILLUSTRATION OF QUALITATIVE WHOLENESS

In Part I of the LIFE FORMS, Schutz elaborated a number of Bergson's conceptions, notably memory-endowed duration, with the help of illustrative diagrams, algebraic notations, and occasional equations. This was a pedagogical device, well suited for his potential Central-European audience. Since they are obviously not suited for a present-day Northamerican audience of strong leanings toward phenomenological orientations, I, as translator of the Bergson manuscripts into English, omitted the eight diagrams and reduced all mathematical-algebraic expositions to ordinary terms [4].

I would not have chosen to discuss this pedagogical device here at all, were it not for the fact that Schutz had considered it a primary means for the demonstration of the points he had to make throughout the long theoretical manuscript of the first part.

By his own gymnasial (high school) and academic training, Schutz was well prepared for illustrating non-quantitative ideas by quantitative means. He may have felt encouraged by Bergson to do so; the latter had stressed the unavoidability of presenting his ideas of the pure quality of duration in a language which, by function and definition, consists of basically quantitative-spatial terms. It may seem, then, that little additional damage could be done to the idea of duration by presenting it not in a language which refers to time in covertly spatial forms but in a language expressly created for the overt reduction of the description of anything to purely quantitative and geometrical signs, that is, to terms of mathematical and algebraic precision. The principle, here, would be the same as that which underlies the construction of ideal types: selection of an extreme form which, in application, will have to be considerably amended.

Schutz did not offer this or any other argument in justification of his diagrams. But, in discussing each of them, he invariably warned his readers not to see them as simplified pictures of the realities of consciousness to which they referred. Being unable to judge whether they would have fulfilled their pedagogical purposes, if the manuscripts had been published at the time, I find them of interest for another reason, a reason not part of Schutz's intentions. The graphs themselves were time continua; some of them formed a series of growing complexity, designed to diagram the changes memory images undergo with growing time distance from the point of their origin. By this graphical conversion of duration into a quasi-mathematical time continuum, Schutz managed, literally, to "lay out in space" what was described by Bergson and him as a purely qualitative manifold in constant flux, remaining forever indivisible. Doing so, he unwittingly turned an academically common pedagogical device into a means of demonstrating the paradoxy of Bergson's paradox; he gave it the most extreme form possible. He effected this by moving from the hidden quantitative-spatial connotations and implications of ordinary language to the artificially created and exclusively quantitative language of mathematics; from first-order spatialization in the guise of everyday language to the second-order spatialization of an "artificial" algebraic symbol system.

I submit that the decision to do this was in full agreement with Bergson's expositions of the characteristics of all language, including the vernacular of everyday life. In this respect, geometrical-algebraic concepts, the products and foundations of one type of thinking in the "scientific stance," represent nothing but the systematic precisioning of one inherent structural feature of everyday language.

If this conception of language is questioned - and I do question it - Schutz's selection of quantitative-geometrical spatialization for illustrative purposes appears as a questionable choice [5].

Granting that nothing can remove the distinction between experiences and talking about them, I cannot concede that it makes no difference what kind of language - or terms of the chosen language - we choose for talking about experiences. By the same token, it is preferable to use the fuzzy and imprecise terms of ordinary language when speaking about the notion of duration. Ordinary words allow the bestowal of meanings upon them which deviate from, or even replace completely, 'official' dictionary definitions. Bergson did not pay much attention to this possibility; yet, it is crucial for explaining that Bergson, or anybody else, could at all attempt to explain duration.

Three years after the publication of Bergson's ESSAI, James pointed forcefully to this in his theory of fringes. Schutz picked up this notion - likely from a secondary source - and viewed it in the context of his discussion of the relationship between "word forms" and "word meaning" (1982: 162, others) [6]. What Schutz called "the Word" designates words, phrases, sentences, and paragraphs of language-in-use. To the individual who thinks, speaks and writes or else hears or reads and comprehends them, they appear with a "penumbra" of meanings which are not subject to dictionary-precise definitions. For the speaking or listening, and often the writing or reading individual, the actual meaning evoked occurs in the fringes which surround the words given in a certain context - this context being both that of the emerging drift or topic of the conversation and that of the given concrete situation in which it takes place.

Fringes occur wherever concepts are formed: "No word exists which would be unambiguous, and no word which is only ambiguous. Word and concept are discrepant just for this reason: it takes the whole complicated apparatus of the activity of reason in order to distil the concept from the word and to force the concept thus gained into a formula for convenience, the technical term" (1982: 143).

In the case of such distillation, the gap between concept and meaning tends toward zero. But it could be argued that zero is reached only in the case of mathematical symbols. By contrast, the gap is at a maximum in poetry. Everything else, obviously, can be found somewhere between these extremes. It is for this reason that, in the case of explaining duration, ordinary language is preferable to algebraic representation.

In theory, Schutz was well aware of the danger of resorting to quasi-mathematical abstraction, or even conceptual abstraction. Refuting the prevailing notion "that abstraction is the existence of pure images of perception," he argued: by "isolating an 'image' from pure duration" without considering what came before and comes after in any Now and Thus, one "abandons the only way of reflection which is adequate to pure duration" (1982: 48). With these remarks, Schutz indicated himself the reason for the sake of which it is desirable to abstain from the algebraization of the conception of duration.

The likening of duration to a quasi-mathematical continuum amounts to the cutting into discrete minute segments of time what is a continuous flow. The same segmentation procedure is applied to the content of experiences occurring in the flow of duration whenever this content itself is segmented into static bits which resemble the isolated 'moments' of a mathematical continuum. Schutz approached such an application when he discussed a simple event taking place in the sphere of somatic experiences: A kind of "stimulus" hits the eye; I reflexively recoil and close the eye, opening it again when nothing further happens. In memory-endowed duration, Schutz explained, "the event presents itself as a series of quality experiences, independent of each other and not reducible to each other." The event itself falls into events which occur in the following sequence: "light ray, pain, feeling blinded, closing eyes, no pain, opening eyes." They "occur absolutely independent of, but turn into, each other; and this next to thousands and thousands of other quality experiences which, together and intermingled, may constitute the respective Now and Thus" (1982: 78).

If these considerations are accepted at face value, they indicate that the total experience of a given Now and Thus consists of "thousands and thousands" of mosaic pieces, a truly atomistic description of the unitary wholeness of the experience itself. Being perfectly aware of this, Schutz added significant correctives to his exposition: The independent events "are merely strung together by the thread of my duration"; the "only thing they have in common is that they are my experiences." Clearly, then, the isolated minute items of experience are united by the unitary I (1982: 78).

It is in no way surprising that Schutz should resort here to the same ego which he introduced as the unifier of the system of analytically separated life forms. However, it evokes great interest to find that he also alluded to a principle of unification which, so to speak, inheres in the multiplicity of isolated events itself. As quoted, he said that they run into each other. And, although in a negative form, he strengthened this notion with the further assertion: "Separated from another by nothing, they are nothing set apart, or distinguished, from other quality experiences" (UM 1925-1927b; see 1982: 78). Doubtlessly, Schutz came to these statements in the attempt at reconciling the form of an atomistic description with the content of the notion of a flowing and coherent duration. Yet, they also can be read as at least rudimentary indications of an understanding of the Gestalt principle, with which he should become acquainted considerably later. At the time, Gestalt psychology itself was in its early stages, and Schutz was unaware of its beginnings. These Beginnings were largely confined to the exploration of perceptions: In a narrower field, the Gestalt psychologists faced up to the same problem of 'whole and parts' which Schutz touches upon on the level of images of experience. Their quite revolutionary contribution, simply, consists in the experimental proof that the so far generally assumed relationship between parts and whole has to be reversed: Where traditional and especially behaviorist psychologists explain any whole, notably a perceptual whole, as the addition of atomistic details, the Gestalt psychologists established the primacy of the whole in perception and eventually in other areas of consciousness and cognition. The whole, or Gestalt, is realized before details can be, and are, gained by some deliberate effort.

It would lead too far afield to attempt here a development of the rudimentary starting points, which can be found in the cited passages of Schutz, to a description of the realization of events in memory-endowed duration in full agreement with the Gestalt principle [7]. The fact remains that Schutz, already in 1925, groped in this direction when he hinted at the possibility of a different treatment of the problem of the parts and the whole within the unity of an experience.

MEMORY IMAGES

The second point of our present considerations concerns Schutz's acceptance of Bergson's conception of memory images. In the nutshell, this conception was based on the distinction between two forms of memory: The first concerns the "recording" of memories, the second their recall. In the first form, memory "records, in the form of memory images, all the events of our daily life as they occur in time; it neglects no detail; it leaves to each fact, to each gesture, its place and date." All these images are "stored up in the spontaneous memory." Thus, "the whole series of our past images remains present with us." This suggests the following comment: Each of these images is like a snapshot produced by a camera which is clicking away in quick succession; it falls, so to speak, into a slide container and can be picked out for viewing whenever needed. This need, in Bergson's terms, is expressed in the second form of memory: the actual recall of specific memory images. This form is "active and motor," and it accepts from the memory images of the first form only "that which can throw light upon and complete in a useful way the present situation" but, likewise, may "inhibit" the occurrence of such images (1896: 92, 97, 114, 97).

This split theory is justified insofar as, obviously, I could not remember anything unless something was 'there' latently and could be brought into consciousness. What this something is, however, is unascertainable in contrast to the existence of a box filled with slides, which can be inspected without looking at any of the pictures on the slides. There is no other access to Bergson's memory images outside of remembering. This, again, means that his memory images as such are as hypothetical and unreachable by introspection as his pure duration. In Schutz's terms, they are artificial ideal-typical constructions, introduced for theoretical convenience.

In a very interesting passage, Bergson dealt with the way in which present "external perception" is intertwined with internal memory: "... our memory directs upon the perception received the memory images which resemble it and which are already sketched out by the movements themselves. Memory thus creates anew the present perception, or rather it doubles this perception by reflecting upon it either its own image or some other memory-image of the same kind.

If the retained or remembered thing will not cover all the details of the image that is being perceived, an appeal is made to the deeper and more distant regions of memory, until other details that are already known come to project themselves upon these details that remain unperceived" (1896: 123).

This passage, which directs itself not only to recall but also the question of recognition of elements of present perceptions as already known in general from past experiences, shows that Bergson tried to keep his theory of first-form memory images intact: What will become the memory image of the present moment, in the case described, is so-to-speak a montage of cut-outs from details of different memory images pertaining to different moments of past experiences.

Schutz accepted the storage theory of memory images: "Remembering a specific event consists in the reproduction of a memory image which has been removed from the flow of our duration." Yet, what is plausible "at face value," demands further scrutiny. The question, "what happens when we remember a specific event of our life," demands an answer which goes beyond Bergson. Thus. Schutz stressed that the identity of past experiences with their memory images is impossible. Since any memory image is produced in inner duration, it must be assumed that it is itself "a kind of combination of all preceding experiences." The first memory image of an event, so to speak, is seen through the filters of re-remembrance because in each interval new experiences have been added to memory." Thus, "my memory does not mechanically register the experiences of my inner duration: ... it integrates them" (1982: 44-45).

Doubtlessly, these considerations aimed at the removal of the dualism of memory images and recall, which Bergson had introduced. If Schutz did not follow them through, so likely because he was not yet in possession of the phenomenological insight into the intentionality of consciousness. Had he been, he would have clearly realized that 'memory images' come only into view as 'object' of an intentional glance backward: the relevances which beset my attention at the present Now, govern the selection of memories of certain past experiences and the more recent experiences through which they are seen on the one hand, and the aspects or moments of these past experiences which come actually into focus on the other hand. Phenomenally, there is no 'memory image' outside of this intentionality. Bergson's two forms are indeed artificial constructions not needed for the phenomenal description of remembering. It is to the credit of Schutz that, at the time, he made a good step toward the elimination of this dualism.

SYMBOLIZATION AND SYMBOL FUNCTION

Next, I will turn to Schutz's uses of the terms function and symbol as he combined them in the term, symbol functions - a highly important concept for the theory of the life forms.

With regard to the term, function, I will confine myself to the remark that Schutz used it operationally - that is, undefined - in a number of unrelated contexts: when he specified it occasionally, so only in relation to the specific case on hand.

By contrast, the term symbol belonged to the central conceptual equipment of Schutz's Bergson project. As such, it warrants a minimum of discussion preliminary to the exposition of the notion of "symbol functions." Most of all, he approached the topic of symbols and symbolization in a highly critical manner. Thus, he pointed out that, in spite of an abundance of literature on the topic, "the problem has been rarely treated in general terms, focusing on cognition as such." In fact, he added, the concept itself "has been treated as given and not in need of further explanation"; the origin of symbol phenomena "was not pursued"; it lies in "pre-scientific spheres" which have been shunned by all investigators (1982: 69-70), Bergson conspicuously not excluded.

Schutz's substantive treatment of symbolization was aimed at making up for this omission. Indeed, one can distinguish a number of observations which can be found again, three decades later, in his masterful essay on "Symbol, Reality and Society" (1955b). Yet, as a whole, his uses of the term, symbol, in the LIFE FORMS were not free of some of the equivocations which were characteristic of the literature in question. He too applied the term, maybe less than others, in an omnibus fashion - as I wrote in my introduction to the LIFE FORMS. That means, the symbol label was attached to any tangible (visible, audible, touchable) object which was intended to be, and understood as, standing for something else. Generally speaking, this covers the immense range between a letter of the alphabet standing for a speech sound and a visible gesture or a material object standing for a most esoteric or sublime idea utterly incomprehensible in or by itself.

Having given these critical conclusions in a general form, I have made the indicated shortcomings sound worse than they are within the context of the manuscripts of the LIFE FORMS. First of all, Schutz himself did not treat the symbol problem "in general terms," and he did not focus on "cognition as such." Rather, he did so in terms of the pre-designed hierarchical scheme of the life forms and focused on cognition within the confines of this framework. The latter was consistent as rational-interpretative system and promised to yield a consistent interpretation of symbols, symbol relations, and symbol functions. But it was not comprehensive; its uppermost stratum was the life form of the thinking I and one half expected that it again would be turned into the foundation of a next-higher layer: that of the thinking I in the scientific and rational-philosophical stance. If the whole served as theory of cognition, so in the sense of leading up to a theory of rational cognition.

Risking repeating myself, I have to point out once more that Schutz's scholarly integrity brought him to the recognition and pursuit of inner-experiential evidence which could not be completely explained in terms of the theoretical scheme and induced him to attempt adaptations of the scheme to all his evidence, but he was not successful in this: The revisions threatened its logical-theoretical consistency. Whatever theory of consciousness resulted from the whole undertaking, it was not comprehensive. On the other hand, I also suspect that some of the highly interesting topical explorations of the three substantive essays of the second part brought not only a deepening or expansion of topics derived from the framework of the first part, but also lead to other topics which transcend this framework [8].

In any case, whatever Schutz's original expectations were, the theory of consciousness underlying, and being compatible with, the theory of the life forms was not comprehensive, not theory of "consciousness as such." Similarly, and in connection with this, the scheme did not, and was not designed to, accommodate an exposition of the "origin of symbol phenomena" in the only sense admissable here. Schutz started the exposition of his symbol theory with the thesis: "Symbol and symbolized are one in the awareness of the life form which precedes the symbol experience" (1982: 54). Even if we consider that this oneness is given already in the 'lowest' life form, pure duration, we are without any idea as to how the 'symbol' originated in its unity with the 'symbolized.' It is postulated as being there in a hidden form. But, the only plausible interpretation of Schutz's theory of symbolization is not that symbols are 'discovered' in but imputed to the "lower life form," actually the flow of experiencing after it has been passed away or stopped and is retrospectively grasped and subjected to interpretation. Symbolization, in my judgment, is always interpretation after the fact. The symbol has no 'existence' outside of interpretations.

When Schutz spoke of symbol relations, he referred to the ideal-typically postulated linkage between two life forms, that is, a quite different interpretation from that of the imposition of meaning through symbolization in everyday life experiences. This theory does not explain the "origin of the symbol" but takes for granted the ability of Man as conscious being to symbolize, that is, to endow meanings to his experiences in retrospective interpretation.

Schutz had been well aware of the fact that symbolization can be carried out only by resorting to language: In this connection, interpretation is the verbalization of past experiences or, in Bergson's terms, lifting these experiences out of inner duration and into the realm of the space-time world. He also knew that this could be done, in the narrower sense, only by resorting to a socially pregiven "symbol system," that of a specific language. But such a system is that of a technical means. Symbolic interpretation of experiences is impossible without the use of language, but the symbol system of this language does not provide such interpretations: they are provided by the experiencing person who resorts to other kinds of symbol systems. In most routine cases of everyday life, such systems are also socially pregiven in the "folkways and mores" as well as the "relative-natural view of the world" of the effective social group to which the person belongs [9]. This is correct only with the conditional amendment: A given individual resorts to socially pregiven interpretative systems 'as understood by him in any concrete case of actual experiences he wishes to interpret.' Next to this, in other cases individuals will refer to their own reference systems; they are personal, resulting from past interpretations of personal experiences and will change with ongoing experiences in one's ongoing life.

All this, if not actually foreseen in the Bergson study, in compatible with Schutz's theory of symbolization offered in it. Yet, he classified as symbol systems at least four different reference systems: that of the formal-official language, one socially pregiven, one largely of any individual's own making, and one theoretically constructed by a social scientist or philosopher. In all four cases, the symbol system has different characteristics and serves different purposes.

I will point to two of them now in the context of the consideration of Schutz's concept of "symbol functions." I will presuppose that the expression refers to 'symbols in use' in cognitive actions of its user(s), that is, in acts of symbolization. This 'subjective' characteristic of symbol functions reached full attention under the heading, "The Symbol Function of the Acting I." This expression allows two interpretations: (a) the symbol function exercised by the acting I, and (b) the symbol function appropriate to the ideal type of the life form of the Acting I.

The distinction is crucial: In the first case, we refer to the acting and experiencing individual who, in interpretative and explanatory efforts, "symbolizes" retrospectively experiences which have passed away. In the second case, the constructor of the ideal type - acting here as theorist, not as uninvolved observer - constructs the contentless form of an ideal-typical "symbol function" which links the ideal type of a higher life form to another such life form which, in the total scheme, is placed directly below It.

It may be unfortunate that Schutz did not work out the important distinctions among the four symbol systems mentioned, and in particular not the distinction between the two symbol functions of the acting I. Instead, he was preoccupied with symbolization as a linkage mechanism between adjacent life forms. Since Ilja Srubar has offered an excellent exposition of this mechanism in chapter 3 of this book, I do not have to discuss it here.

While the mechanism became obsolete with the whole theory of the life forms, Schutz touched upon various aspects of symbolization as an actual achievement of the I which interprets its own experiences. For the viable development of these aspects, however, we will have to turn to his later work.

MEANING AND THE SUBJECT-OBJECT DICHOTOMY

Introducing the last topic of this chapter, I will mention that Schutz, during his secondary and academic training, had absorbed a number of philosophical formulae not only for dealing with theoretical, epistemological, and ontological problems, but also for laying out maps of reality. Among them was the subject-object dichotomy, widely taken as self-evident. Epistemologically, it meant the confrontation of the cognitizing ego or, by Kant, of consciousness in general, with the objects of cognition. what could be less unambiguous than the distinction between the thinker and the object which he perceives and about which he reflects, or between cognition and its content? Was it not this which Husserl had in mind, when he formulated the slogan, "Back to the Things"?

The antinomic form of the dichotomy lends itself to manifold specifications. Many cognitive terms could be split by the simple expedient of prefacing them by the dichotomic adjectives, subjective and objective. In the Bergson manuscripts, Schutz made use of this expedient. Thus, he concerned himself conspicuously with a problem which he considered equally relevant for the heterogeneous areas of language, the arts, and the sciences: "the problem of subjective and objective meaning" (1982: 68). He posed this problem not only in the first part of his study but also in the three essays making up the second part. In my exposition, I will rely mainly on a section of "Meaning Structures of Literary Art Forms," which I titled "The Life Form of the Speaking I: Speaker and Listener" (1982: 160-162).

In it, language is announced as "a life form of man who lives in space, time, and Thou relation" [10]. "Common to all of us," it "comprises all objects which you and I can apperceive simply by naming them." Their names are linguistic signs or symbols - terms which, in Schutz's vocabulary of the period, are used quite synonymously. In this "language permeated reality" occurs nothing, including events and past, present or future actions, which language could not seize and which are not preformed by "the Word," that is, the spoken language used in communication between persons. Any language, as shared system of communication, forms an "objective meaning context" which the users of the language must "subjectivize," that is, give a meaning.

With Max Weber, Schutz considered communication as a form of social action, that is, the action of an individual which directs himself intentionally to another individual - here in order to elicit a response. Apparently for reasons of methodological simplification, this conception of social action has been based on an incomplete scheme of interaction, expressed by Schutz in the juxtaposition of speaker and listener. The assumption behind this foreshortened treatment is that, should the listener answer, he becomes the speaker and the initial speaker the listener. The reversal of the roles does not add anything to the initial scheme; but their repeated alternation yields a pattern of dialogue.

In Schutz's exposition of the process of communication, meaning is suspended between subjective and objective connotations. By subjective meaning, according to the manuscript on the "Meaning Structures of Language," he understood "the meaning posited by the I" - that is, the I as the speaker - "which confronts the Thou" - the listener - "as objective meaning, already posited and now in need of interpretation." This objective meaning is embodied in "the Word," that is, the spoken word as denoting an object of whatever kind, and thus as "objective meaning content" (1982: 142, 143).

In may be remarked in passing that, in this statement, the terms, subjective and objective meanings, could be reformulated without the qualifying adverbs: We could as well speak of meaning and denotation, respectively. This would be consistent with phenomenological usage, in which meaning is a subjective term by definition. By contrast, and clearly so in general usage, denotation refers to the "objective meaning" a term has obtained in the context of a linguistic system. It is understood that this terminological correction does in no way change the underlying object-subject dichotomy itself.

Schutz explained that the speaker subjectivizes the Word in the act of "positing meaning." He "appropriates" the words he chooses in order to convey to others the meaning he has in mind. Such appropriation amounts to giving the language terms in question "a special, unique, a new meaning for the speaker." He intends to communicate this new meaning to the person he addresses. The terms used belong to the "objectively meaning-endowed material of the language as such," its denotations, but are integrated "into the subjectively meaning-endowed context of speech" (1982: 160).

The listener, on his part, relates what he hears only to "the objective material" of the language. His initial interpretation of the words heard occurs "according to the scheme of language which he attitudinally adopted and which is familiar to him." The ensuing process is the reversal of that chosen by the speaker. The latter, in a way, translates the intended meaning into objective words. The listener attempts to comprehend the denotative connotations of the words spoken [11]; this achieved, "he tries to understand the meaning which the speaker meant"; he translates objective words into meaning (1982: 161).

Initially, then, the listener's position is this: He "does mean nothing; he does not want to provide a new meaning." Thus, he is not even aware of the fact "that his meaning interpretation implicitly comprises subjectivation." For him, "the word heard is and remains an objective meaning which is integrated into the objective meaning context of language, and vice versa. Not the listener, only the speaker means something with the word; not the speaker, only the listener interprets it" (1982: 161).

There is, then, a discrepancy between what speaker and listener comprehend when involved in speaking or listening and the description of speaking and listening by Schutz. He has established himself in the position of "the third observer"; only from his point of view "is the act of listening a subjectivation of the objective meaning context of language." Yet, for purposes of the theoretical description of the observed relationship between speaker and listener, Schutz underlined once more that "'subjective meaning' shall always be taken as the intended meaning (thus of the speaker) and 'objective meaning' as the meaning to be interpreted (thus by the listener)" (1982: 161).

Toward the end of these considerations, Schutz remarked that "the speaker is never only speaker but also listener." While this statement offers a convenient opening for the treatment of the reversal of the roles of speaker and listener and, in fact, of the reciprocity of dialogue, Schutz did not avail himself of this opportunity, Rather, he used it for appraising the chances of an understanding arising from the speaker-listener configuration. He pointed to the significant fact that "for everyone in any kind of language, each word is colored differently and surrounded by a specific aura of significance and meaning content." In other words, the "objective meaning" of words in use is subjectively colored by unrecognized meanings located in their subjectively unique penumbra. Schutz concluded that, for this pertinent reason, "in the linguistic sphere alone, a complete understanding of a meaning context posited by the speaker (subjective meaning) cannot be established in the meaning interpretation carried out by the listener (objective meaning)." Full understanding is not possible: "Within language alone, understanding remains an (even though asymptotic) approximation between subjective and objective meaning, between intended and interpreted meaning" (1982: 162). In other words: the dichotomy cannot be completely obliterated, at least not as long as only verbal communication is involved.

The introduction of an "aura" surrounding words is quite relevant. In the "Meaning Structures of Language," Schutz formulated the same idea and re-acknowledged its originator: "... the word as such, namely, as objective meaning content, is always logically inexact. As imaginary object, it leads its own life (in the twilight) of the subjective positing of meaning and the - again subjective - meaning interpretation ... It is surrounded by a penumbra which the concept penetrates only with great effort. In this context, James coined the brilliant term, 'fringes of the word' " (1982: 143). This notion served Schutz as argument for the impossibility of complete linguistic understanding and, in this sense, against the possibility of the complete removal of the object-subject dichotomy. By the same token, however, it undermines the conception of the objectivity of language in action. Such objectivity exists solely in grammar texts and dictionaries, that is, in a kind of formalization of language which occurs on a similar level as that of the formalism of mathematics and of logic. It is for this reason that Schutz's basic treatment of language in actual communication, executed in terms of the concepts of speaker and listener, appears unsatisfactory. The conversion of both into terms fitting the subject-object dichotomy prevents the treatment of communication as an in principle reciprocal affair, as dialogue in process and in progression.

The silent assumption that the incomplete scheme of speaker and listener becomes complete with the reversal of the roles is at variance with observed and observable facts. What Schutz explained, at best, is the first step, the initiation of communication. The person addressed initially "means nothing"; he must make sense of the words heard. But he cannot answer unless he has given the message received a meaning - excluding here the intermediary case of partial failure to get the denotative connotation of what has been said and therefore, to replace the response by a request for clarification. The speaker who initiated the communication does not listen to the words of the response without meaning anything. He has already posited a meaning with and through his initial statement, and he is set to hear the response in the light of this intended meaning. By the same token, the original listener, becoming the speaker after listening to the first statement of the person who addressed him, means something with his response. From here on, the exchange continues not in the two-step manner indicated by Schutz. If communication is successfully initiated, the effort to comprehend the linguistically "objective material" is largely absorbed in the effort to understand "meanings meant" by either of the participants.

In other words, in the same fashion in which Weber's term, social action, demands expansion to the term of social interaction, so does the notion of the subjectivity of meaning demand its expansion to intersubjectivity.

These critical remarks contain nothing which could not be found in Schutz's later writings and, in fact, have been derived from them. In the Bergson manuscripts, he was still using the subject-object dichotomy in the older sense of a clear and self-evident separation of the Subjective, as that which issues from an individual's interests, motives, and interpretations (meanings), from the Objective as that which exists independent from subjects and forms its own ontological realm. Later, when Schutz had come to a clear understanding of the phenomenological conception of intentionality, he found the subject-object dichotomy in the older form misconceived and misleading. But since not even the philosophical phenomenologists have found a linguistic substitute for the terms, he resigned himself to continue their use. Forthwith, however, he took care to show what the words, objective and subjective, stood for in a given concrete case. Thereby, he made clear that these words are ambivalent, that is, gain different meanings in different contexts - a fact which is hidden when they are used without further explanation. Thus, in 1958 he defined subjective meaning for sociological purposes as "the meaning which an action has for the actor or which a relation or situation has for the person or persons involved therein." By contrast, "objective meaning is the meaning which the same action, relation, or situation has for anybody else, be it a (listening HRW) partner or observer in everyday life, the social scientist, or the philosopher." This would seem to be in agreement with the interpretation of the difference between speaker and listener, as advanced, more than thirty years earlier. However, in 1958, Schutz warned his readers that this "terminology is unfortunate" and that the term objective meaning "is obviously a misnomer, insofar as the so-called 'objective' interpretations are, in turn, relative to the particular attitudes of the interpreters and, therefore, in a certain sense, 'subjective' " (CP II: 275).

It should be properly noted that Schutz included among the interpreters both social scientists and philosophers insofar as they offer interpretations of human conduct as observed by them from the perspectives of their sociological or philosophical approaches. In consequence, he insisted that, for sociological purposes, the term 'the subjective point of view' designates nothing but the way in which the direct participants in any kind of social situation see the situation; by contrast, 'the objective point of view' is nothing but the view from which a detached observer sees the same situation [12]. Neither of these two points of view is in itself superior to the other. The subjective viewpoint is the 'correct' one for the involved social actor(s) who pursue(s) his (their) actual purposes according to his (their) systems of relevance; the objective viewpoint is the correct one for sociologists who make their observation "for the sake of knowing" and thereby follow their own theoretical system of relevances which - ideally - is that of their discipline.

While the position explained in the preceding paragraph resulted from Schutz's acceptance of the principles of Max Weber's methodology, he also made significant steps forward in the realm of the phenomenal-psychological interpretation of those inter-actional involvements of individuals in concrete social situations. Here, he was largely inspired by Husserl. What, in the LIFE FORMS, had been seen by him in terms of the subjective-objective dichotomy of meanings and their presentation, respectively interpretation, by speaker and listener, was superseded by his theory of mundane intersubjectivity. Thus, he offered his revealing considerations of Husserl's "communicative common environment," his own "general thesis of the alter ego" and of the "we-relationship" (CP III: 27-30, CP I: 172-175, 1932: 181-182). Together, these considerations form the core of Schutz's conception of the life-world as the rootbed and field of its continuous re-creation and re-confirmation [13].

PROBLEM-CONTINUITY

One may be inclined to place side-by-side topics appearing both in the unfinished drafts of 1925-1928 and in DER SINNHAFTE AUFBAU of 1932; the immediate impression will be that of a contrast in consistency and execution which in itself explains why Schutz discarded the first and wrote the second. From this comparative angle, nothing more would have to be said. However, after careful reflection, the first impression yields to the recognition of at least two definitely 'positive' factors. One is that the common themes in both are responses to the same problems. For some, this may count little; for me, it counts much [14]. The significance of the second factor ought to be more obvious. It concerns the substance of Schutz's first attempts at answering the problems posed. Basically, these make out the primary thematic of the next three chapters of this study. Confining myself here to the present chapter, I will highlight my expositions of the four thematic points from this angle. (1) In contrast to the pedagogical use of atomizing quasi-mathematical expositions, Schutz stressed the necessity of establishing the unity of consciousness and groped for it in the direction of both gestalt-theoretical and egological principles. (2) In spite of seemingly accepting Bergson's dualistic theory of memory, he moved toward a unitary theory of remembering. (3) In his treatment of the "symbol function," he made significant attempts to respond to the problem of symbolization; but his efforts suffered most from being tied to the notion of a linkage mechanism in the ideal-typical scheme of the hierarchy of life forms. (4) Schutz made the first steps toward overcoming the traditional connotation of the subject-object dichotomy by treating it in terms of meaning positing and interpreting in conversations: both cases center on the "subjectivation" of words used. He found this possible because - in contrast to Bergson - he was aware of the "penumbra" or "aura" surrounding words heard or spoken by persons communicating with one another. If he did not follow this through, so because he was still entangled in the traditional subject-object dichotomy.

In none of the four cases did Schutz reach the phenomenological clarity he displayed in the AUFBAU. It must be kept in mind that between the two projects lies an almost two-year period of the most intensive study of Husserl's available writings. In his first study, he tried for phenomenological answers to his thematic problems; but the means at his disposal were inadequate.

CHAPTER 7

SOMATIC FEELINGS OF LIFE: AN IMPORTANT CONTRIBUTION

In Chapter 3, Ilja Srubar has given a clear description of Schutz's system of the six life forms. It would be unnecessary to refer to this system again, were it not for at least two attempts of Schutz to expand or amend the scheme. Although he did not follow them through systematically, they are of great interest for us. To begin with: While inconspicuously mentioned in Schutz's outline for the study, their significance for it emerged only during its execution. Thus, Schutz had to grant them the status of separate topics of the magnitude of the individual life forms. In fact, at one point or other, he called them life forms too, even though he refrained from integrating them systematically into the six-layer scheme as such.

In itself, the expansion of the scheme from six to eight layers would have been a secondary matter. Although the six presented convey the impression not only of a systematic and well-organized structure but also that of a closed system, Schutz himself called the selection arbitrary and stated that "an infinite number of such planes of consciousness of life forms can be projected into the totality of the real ego." Which of all possible life forms were placed in the scheme, "remains a question of purpose" (1982: 21); it depended on the theoretical objectives of the study.

As long as we consider the life form scheme relevant in itself, we would have to ascertain the place which Schutz intended to give each of them in his hierarchical scheme and find out how well they fitted into it in terms of the criteria Schutz had set up for their linkage and sequence. But this, again, becomes a secondary point in light of the fact that Schutz did not carry the conception of the life forms over into his mature work, in contrast to various other conceptions he had gained during the Bergson period. In this sense, the scheme became part of a stage Schutz had outgrown in the same way in which he had outgrown - years earlier - his neoKantian stage.

Needless to say, this would apply to any addition to the six life forms, provided they were successfully integrated into the scheme. However, as I found out after a painstaking analysis of Schutz's attempts in this direction, the two I hinted at could not be fitted in [1]. This, in itself, could be discarded as a stab in the wrong direction. However, this failure is of interest on account of the reasons which motivated Schutz to risk it and for the conclusions which have to be drawn from it. The purpose of the ideal-typical scheme and the purposes of the attempted additions did not co-incide; the attempts were directed upon objectives transcending the life-form conception.

SOMATIC EXPERIENCES

The two additions envisaged by Schutz were of quite different character: one referred to the life of the body, the other to the existence of the ego. In this chapter, I will concentrate on the first one, which Schutz introduced as "the life form of the somatic feeling of life." In some way or other, it is linked both to memory-endowed duration and the acting I (1982: 83). Abstaining here from discussing his suggestion to place it between these two life forms, which comes as a surprise, I shall turn to the general characterization of the "somatic feeling of life." With it, Schutz placed a theme of great phenomenological importance on the agenda.

In a remarkable attempt at catching the retentions of quality experiences of a simple activity, Schutz showed that the conventional elements of a description of this activity will not do at all when I turn my attention on my actual sensations while, for instance, writing the capital letter A. There is no sheet on top of the table, no pen held between fingers and set on the sheet, and no hand and forearm moving the pen across a segment of the paper. Rather, there are quality experiences of a visual or tactile kind, color differences, feelings of pressures issuing from nerve endings in parts of the skin, tensions located in certain muscular tissues, sensations of movements against some resistance, and whatever. Again, the description of these sensations resorts immediately to terms I have learned in physiology classes; they are still more remote from what is going on than my primitive resorting to the thing-language of everyday life: paper, pen, finger, forearm, etc. All this pre-existing 'knowledge' rushes into consciousness when attention is switched from the intention-in-action, the writing of the letter A, to the description of the sensations, quality impressions, during its execution. The latter, immediately, becomes interpretation of quality experiences in thing-terms; these experiences are laid out in space - this-sheet-here - and in time - this-hand-moving-now and can now be sorted out into three distinguishable groupings: the intention-in-action, the objects perceived (seen and/or felt), and the physiological sensations of the moving hand (1982: 74-78, 83-87).

Excluding the intentional sphere from further consideration, Schutz investigated the elementary characteristics of the used object and the using hand. He found that, when one views these characteristics retrospectively in memory, there is no basic difference between the pen perceived and my hand perceived: On this level, "no quality experience acquires a privileged rank - not even that of the body" (1982: 76). Yet, common sense emphatically privileges perceptions and sensations directed upon and issuing from one's own body. On principle, then, the privileged position of the body must be given its due. This occurs by another turn of attention. In a deliberate effort, we can "divest ourselves from all sensory perceptions, quality experiences, memory images," etc., thereby making it easier to "turn our attention to the phenomenon of duration." This done, we still retain an awareness of our "I," even if "not in the sense of pure duration," that is, in the psycho-phenomenal sense: "But every breath of my chest, every heartbeat is mine, belongs to me. It is my heart which beats, my chest which raises and falls ... We may call this I-consciousness of the body the feeling of life, the feeling of existing." This, it must be understood, is not a matter of knowledge: "Basically, I do not know anything about my existence. But I know that I breathe," etc. This is an "essential mode" of my being; I "come to know" this "only by cognition" (1982: 76-77).

In this "I-consciousness of the body," we are facing a most challenging attempt at bringing "somatic feelings" into the realm of phenomenal considerations. I will return to it later in order to clarify how Schutz intended to fit it into his reasoning about the life forms as a unitary complex of the structure of consciousness. To do this, it will be necessary to turn our attention to another of the additions suggested by Schutz.

UNITY UNDER STRAIN

In one part of his introduction to LIFE FORMS, Schutz wrote that "a particular stance of the I to the world" manifests itself in each of the life-worldly "planes of consciousness." Single life forms, then, are "always only a selected part of the total I." In this context, finally, he referred to "the life form of the I" (1982: 21). In the text of the first part of the study itself, he returned to this topic, apparently reducing the general scope of the initial announcement to specifics. He explained: "If one starts with the most originary experience of the I, when inquiring into the significance of I consciousness, the content of this experience reduces itself to the experience of unity. Posited unity is addended by the awareness of pure duration as an expanded life form." A few paragraphs later, Schutz re-enforced this statement by another reference to "the primary I as unity (beyond pure duration) which, in a manner of speaking, has been posited as mathematical point of origin" (1982: 52-53).

In their shortness, these statements make it difficult to ascertain (a) what Schutz was driving at, and (b) whether he was fully aware of the apparent contradiction between the seemingly ego-accentuated formulations of "the total I" and "originary experience of the I" on the one hand, the methodological-ideal-typical formulation of the "life form of the I" and the still more formalized notion of the "primary I ... as mathematical point of origin" on the other. Without speculating as to how Schutz would have dealt with these apparently unreconcilable formulations, had he gone over his first draft, I will confine myself to saying that we are dealing here with a strain in his system of the life forms. It was created in the attempt to integrate the experiencing I into it, and seemingly did not disappear with the expedient of calling this I a life form and anchoring it as "primary I" in the same sphere of "irrational abstractions which cannot be experienced," such as pure duration, pure apperceptive images, pure awareness, and pure memory; all of them cannot possibly "present themselves as life forms to the memory-endowed I" (1982: 52) [2].

Since Schutz became aware of the strain in his theory of the life forms (see note 2), and in fact did not develop the idea of a "life form of the I" into an integrated part of the system, I conclude that he could not remove the tension between the "experiencing I" and the ideal-typical scheme. The principle of theoretical consistency called for the reduction of this I to the terms of the scheme, but the I as concrete ego resisted the attempt. This, to me, appears as the most pertinent reason why Schutz eventually decided to give up the whole project.

THE I AS EXPERIENCER AND ITS SOMATIC FEELINGS

Early in the essay on "Meaning Structures of Language," Schutz offered maybe the clearest formulation of the purpose of his project: It was "to order and integrate" the "experiences of the indivisible I through the construction of a series of auxiliary hypotheses, which I called 'life forms'." With this statement, he made clear that this "invisible I" stood outside the theoretical scheme and that the latter was subservient to it in that it was a methodological means for theorizing about this I. And when he explained that the hierarchical system of the life forms with their quasi-developmental progress from the lowest to the highest stages of consciousness is "only serviceable when we assume that we all live in them simultaneously" (1982: 126, 59), he weakened our confidence in it considerably. How adequate to its subject matter can even an ideal-typical scheme be when it replaces experienced simultaneity by step-by-step stages? Is the blanket of analytic abstraction really big enough to cover this discrepancy?

Schutz's primary concern was to develop an I-centered theory of consciousness. We do his central efforts more justice when we set the attempts at integrating the ego into the system of life forms aside as misguided and, therefore, bound to fail, concentrating instead on that which Schutz had to offer as his egological orientation in its own terms. After all, he had come to Bergson not in order to make exercises in the ideal-typical method, but in order to find the proper psychological foundations for Weber's 'subjective' theory of action and understanding; its irrevocable starting point and center was the actor as a being who sees meaning in his conduct and his experiences. In phenomenal terms, the I and the Thou as the other I were of prime relevance to him.

After these considerations, I will return to the theme of the "somatic feelings of life." Since the concrete human I is inseparable from its body - or, rather, since both are one - somatic feelings are part of the experiences of the I. It is of interest to find out how Schutz linked the two together. Explaining that the "somatic feelings of life" appeared in his earlier expositions artificially separated from all that which is experienced in duration, he made the following correction: "The unity of the experiencing I contains both experiences as one: pure duration and pure somatic feeling of life; élan vital, to use Bergson's related term. We experience everything in duration as well as in the rhythm of somatic processes. Thanks to our awareness of their regularity, our breathing and our heartbeats create a division of the indivisible, a discrete arrangement in the manifold of duration. In the latter, everything somatic is quality experience. All awareness of duration is harnessed by the periodicalizing rhythm of the somatic feeling of life" (1982: 77).

Leaving Bergson's élan vital aside, we have here another confirmation of the view that the "unity of the experiencing I," in Schutz's terms, cannot be reduced to a life form: This I is the experiencer of what is described as falling into the realms of the different life forms, and in particular also of all somatic feelings. - But the most significant part of the quotation pertains to the idea that the most basic and ever present somatic feelings, breathing and heartbeat, "harness" duration by their periodicity. We may say that, to use a coarse analogy: they form a dual metronome ticking time intervals into the mere qualitative continuity of the flow of inner duration [3]. Needless to say, this changes the whole complexion of Bergson's conception of pure duration. About this I shall speak after clarifying what Schutz meant by somatic feelings.

He considered all somatic feelings to be feelings of somatic "movement" of four basic kinds: (1) the spontaneous and rhythmically recurring somatic functions of breathing and heartbeat; (2) occasional spontaneous reactions to external stimuli, such as the blinking of the eye lid in response to an approaching outer object; (3) the spontaneously given bodily sensations in cases in which parts or the whole of the body are moved by an outside agency: the finger resting on a pendulum and following its swing or the child sitting on a swing pushed by the mother; and (4) the somatic sensations which accompany the execution of any deliberate movement in the course of physical activities of any kind and description. Schutz was particularly interested in the third and fourth of these forms, which he juxtaposed to each other as the "moved body" and the "moving body," the one accidental, the other issuing from an act of will. But his whole analysis of the variations of somatic movements and experiences is a genuine contribution to the phenomenological understanding of the human body as the somatic substratum of human experience; it should be read with special care (see 1982: 76-96).

The difference between the moved and the moving body, then, is the following: In the first case, the sensation of movement is induced by an outside agency: the body is an 'object' being moved by it. In the second case, the somatic feelings issue from muscular activities which are induced by ego's decision to act: in this sense, the body is "subject" of its own movement; it becomes the instrument of the acting I.

Like the most elementary somatic functions, the moved body becomes accessible to consciousness retrospectively. But: heartbeat, etc. evoke inner-somatic sensations; in principle, the moved body does not evoke such sensations. Whatever sensations issue from its being moved are evoked by an external agency - whether we think of a baby rocked in its mother's arms, a person riding an airplane, or a boy falling from a tree. In all cases, there will be a sensation of being-moved. This sounds like a tautology; however, when we amend this statement to being-moved-through-a-stretch-of-space, we understand that "being-moved" opens up a sensory lane toward the experience of space. I will call this an incipient feeling of spatiality, a rudimentary feeling of space [4].

Schutz realized this clearly. We will understand the true significance of his notion when we turn from the moved body to his conception of the "moving body": It provides somatic feelings and sensations of movement which are evoked by deliberations and which can be recognized most clearly in retrospection. Schutz wrote "that we 'know' our body also in the sphere of the somatic feeling of life when it, respectively one of its organs, starts to act." The talk about organs which start to act indicates that Schutz did not speak of inner organs (heart, lung, etc.) but rather of legs and feet, of arms and hands. However, Schutz corrected this formulation drastically when he explained: "I know about my finger only if I want to lift it and start doing so. This is an 'act of will' and already in Schopenhauer's definition, 'an act of consciousness which transforms itself immediately into a bodily movement' " (1982: 80).

Exemplifying this, Schutz resorted to the "act of will" of writing something. Such an act could be seen phenomenologically as an "act of consciousness" and thus in terms of the writer's intention to convey meanings, offering them for interpretation to a specific person or a specific group of persons, or to an anonymous public as imagined by the writer. Within the essay on "Meaning Structures of Literary Art Forms," Schutz offered an excellent exposition of this aspect in its complications, variations, and ramifications (1982: 158-179). In the present context, however, he concerned himself with what usually is taken for granted: the execution of the intention, the "act of writing" in the narrow technical sense as working with writing utensils, their purposive manipulation with the help of deliberate "bodily movements." The external course of such an act can be observed and described by another person in the same manner in which its final product, say a written page, can be read by others without reference to the writer-actor who wrote it. But here Schutz was not concerned with such description; he concentrated on the inner effects of bodily movements, here those occurring while writing, typing, etc., for the writer and, if describable, so only by her or him.

It is by now understood that such description can only issue from self-observation, that is, by stopping the act of working (writing) and concentrating attention in a retrospective glance on the experience of writing just-passed-away. Doing so, Schutz wrote, I will grasp two "experiences of my inner duration": "the visual quality image of the 'writing hand' as well as the somatic experience of muscular tension." The flowing movement, thus observed, "is without residue dissolved in memory-endowed duration. Yet the somatic feeling of life - if not dissolved in quality images of duration - remains as residue" (1982: 83, 91, 90).

The notion of somatic feelings as "residues" fits well with Schutz's likening them to Bergson's élan vital, a term meaning a universal driving force of life which preserves the freedom of the evolvement of species and individuals [5]. By the way, in a different manner, William James had hit on something similar to Schutz's somatic feelings. A man of extraordinary intuition and introspective power, he knew better than anyone else to catch glimpses of his own consciousness. He offered us the following immediate evidence: "Whenever my introspective glance succeeds in turning round quickly enough to catch one of these manifestations of spontaneity in the act, all it can ever feel distinctly is some bodily process, for the most part taking place within the head" (1890 I: 300).

This is a remarkable passage. At the time, James was unaware of Bergson's notion that "pure duration" is inaccessible to observation. Like him, he had to face up to his inability to introspectively detect "any purely spiritual element at all." But unlike him, he nevertheless came up with an introspective catch: the feeling of "some bodily process." He sensed the physiological process, which he 'knew' - on the strength of scientific theory - must needs go on and carry what he had named the stream of consciousness. Trying to grasp spontaneous consciousness in the act, he reached right through it and, instead, discovered "cephalic motions" which are "the portions of my innermost activity of which I am most distinctly aware." There were "dim portions" which James could not define. We do not at all have to follow him in the hypothetical suggestions that they could turn out not to be different from the distinct ones and that, therefore, "our entire feeling of spiritual activity ... is really a feeling of bodily activities." He himself was not willing to "pledging ourselves in any way to adopt this hypothesis" (1890 I: 301-302). Bowing to the wisdom of this cautionary clause, I too will refrain from speculating as to what the nature of James's "dim portions" may have been.

Speaking in phenomenal-psychological terms, I can confidently state that James introspectively discovered immediate evidence for the existence of a sphere of somatic sensations which Schutz, later, rediscovered and designated appropriately as "somatic feelings of life." However, it needs to be pointed out that Schutz's rediscovery was not a replication of James's findings. Where James had glanced somatic sensations of an immensely subtle nature, Schutz did point to the more tangible evidence of heartbeat, breathing, and sensory feelings issuing from bodily movements, James may have come upon the ultimate limits of introspection along somatic lines. Schutz, on the contrary, seemed to have opened up a whole field of phenomenal and phenomenological investigation.

SOMATIC EXPERIENCES OF THE EXTERNAL WORLD

The ten sections, in which Schutz treated the topic of the somatic feeling of life directly or which formed its immediate context, cover about half of the large first part of his LIFE FORM AND MEANING STRUCTURE. This is noteworthy for two reasons. First, it shows that the topic itself was of such importance for Schutz that he developed it in great detail and demonstrated its significance for the topics which followed it, comprising the "acting I" and its "symbol functions [6]." Second, the twin theme of the "somatic sensation of life" and the "Knowledge of the moving body" appear in the general outline for the study (see Appendix 1) as titles of the first section of a chapter on "The Acting I." Hints at a carry-over into other sections exist. But they do in no way prepare a reader like me for the actual significance it should gain in the execution of the project. It can hardly be doubted that it gained this significance only in the course of Schutz's explorations of memory, meaning, and symbol relations [7].

Having read Schutz's considerations of somatic feelings of life and their ramifications with other aspects of human existence, I do not hesitate to state that they stand out more than anything else included in this unfinished study. They exist as a result of his attempts to back up an ideal-typical framework by concrete phenomenal-psychological evidence. His investigations, in this and a few other respects, were made in the vein of Bergson's work; they are compatible with that of James. Through them, he demonstrated that he was able to use the introspective method. Obviously, he had absorbed it from Bergson's writings; like the latter, he did not make it thematic.

What is the gist of his findings about somatic feelings?

Somatic feelings, as substratum of the ongoing life processes in all life forms, gain a particular significance in Schutz's treatment of the acting I. They issue from the functions of the body and enter awareness "only as functional context." Schutz explained that one is experiencing his body "only in movement." In a broader context, this means that all my experiencing is embedded in some kind of somatic sensations, which may go unnoticed but may also enter awareness: arousal of emotions is accompanied by an acceleration of my heartbeat whose sensations force themselves upon my attention; an experience makes me blush, a somatic process which I cannot help sensing as both a tension in my heart region and in my face; other experiences make me pale, I practically feel how the blood is drained from my face; fear makes me tremble - all sensations which I can hide neither from myself nor from others. I experience and become aware of the "functional context" of somatic feelings most conspicuously in states of emotion; but they are with me in any other waking state, be it spontaneously living-along or deliberate activity (based on 1982: 76-81).

Forgoing further details which could be added to my earlier sketch of basic aspects of somatic feelings, I will concentrate on the crucial point of Schutz's findings: his appraisal of the role such feelings play in my recognition of the world outside of my consciousness. While all sensory organs are gates to this outside world, the impressions produced by them remain inside myself and do not change their meaning whether we explain them in terms of Berkeley's solipsism or that of a rugged materialism. To the sense of touch, however, accrues a significance which makes it particularly difficult to opt for the former even though without proving conclusively the truth of the latter. It brings, as Schutz said, "the continual experience of the boundaries of the body," not in the least by providing "points of contact with surrounding matters." These contacts may be accidental, so when I bump into an object I failed to notice. To gain their full significance, however, they must be deliberate; that is, they must be experiences of the acting I. Thereby, the body is not merely experienced "as functional context" of internal somatic processes but "in functional context," that is, the context of deliberate activities. The interpretative conversion of such experiences into 'symbolic'-linguistic accounts leads to the recognition of the body "as something expanded, extensive, as body in space": "What is performed here is the miracle of the inclusion of extension into the intensive world of experience." This "transformation takes place because this experience is necessarily and exclusively reinterpreted, by and for the acting I, as an experience in space. This opens up access to the world of extension; it alone mediates the experience of space and therewith of time and of external objects." As actor, and only as actor, do I "step out of the non-dimensional manifoldedness of qualities and enter into the discontinuity of heterogeneous space, filled with quantities" (1982: 87-88).

In this statement, Schutz confined himself to dealing with the somatic experience of space, adding the experience of time to it without further ado. In doing so, he confined himself to the symbolization of time in the language of the conceptual reinterpretation of the world as naively experienced. Following Bergson, he considered clock time as being "laid out" in spatial terms: time is a succession of equi-distanced discrete points along a mathematical continuum. I am referring to this time conception as the spatialization of time or duration. Again according to Bergson, inner-time experiences have nothing to do with this spatialized time conception in everyday language and in scientific thinking. Yet, Schutz distantiated himself from Bergson's extreme position. At least, he indicated one point from which a transition from inner time to outer time could be made; much in the sense in which he had indicated the possibility of a transition from somatic feelings to the comprehension of extension and outer space. In a passage, quoted before, he said: "Thanks to our awareness of their regularity, our breathing and our heartbeat create a division of the indivisible, a discrete arrangement in the manifold of duration. ... All awareness of duration is harnessed by the periodicalizing rhythm of the somatic feeling of life." In confirmation of Bergson's thesis of the spatialization of time, the language used by him in the first sentence, speaking of "division" and "discrete arrangement," suggests strongly a laying-out of rhythmic somatic experiences in space. But the second sentence no less strongly indicates that this spatial language appears with an intent which is the opposite of that of ordinary language: it does not convert time into space; it hides genuine duration behind the disguise of spatial terms. The notion of the harnessing of the awareness of duration "by the periodicalizing rhythm of the somatic feeling of life," to my understanding, indicates that a non-spatialized awareness of time is imposed upon pure duration by certain somatic feelings which, thereby, create an experiential bridge from inner to outer time experiences with a direct approach instead of the 180-degree-turn of the cloverleaf access lane of conceptual spatialization [8].

It may not be amiss to add here that the foregoing paragraph reflects the paradox of which Bergson spoke: the necessity of speaking about inner experiences and inner duration with the help of a language whose terms and structure form a matrix of presentation. The latter is 'made for' cognitive-terminological dealings with objects and perceived relations among them; and for structuring the outer world of our everyday experiences. The discrepancy between experienced (inner) time and measured time itself is part of the paradox.

Therefore, it could be concluded that finding "a transition from inner time to outer time" means a maybe quixotic attempt at solving the linguistic paradox. However, it must be kept in mind that the person who feels feelings and senses inner experiences and the person speaking about his or her feelings and sensations is the same person. That is what Schutz meant when stressing the "unitary I" which "exists simultaneously in all" life forms (1982: 79). Conceptual thinking itself is a particular kind of self-experience, and speaking in exchange with others is intersubjective experience. And that means, phenomenologically, both are in part floating with and in part steering through the uniquely personal undercurrent of their "stream of consciousness" - but with a significant difference: In meaningful conversation, two streams of consciousness interfere with each other, intermingle, and thus each becomes what it would not have become in the course of solitary thinking. The cognitive effects of the dialogue are accompanied by effects issuing from the fact that the exchange itself is a human experience shared by two.

I am throwing in these remarks - which will have to be pursued and developed with great care in future investigations - in order to indicate that the paradoxical contrast between language and expression of inner experience appears only when seen from a purely linguistic perspective. Certainly, immerse differences between experiencing inner feelings and experiencing one's own cognitive efforts or experiencing rational-cognitive interchanges remain, but they are not as forbidding as it appears in Bergson's antinomic presentation. Thus, I can maintain my suggestion that at least some resemblance of a transition from inner to outer time can be found and that Schutz moved in this direction.

As stated before, it must be assumed that somatic feelings constitute a substratum of human life in all its manifestations. My expositions, as truncated as they were, ought to have conveyed a sufficient idea of Schutz's treatment of them and of the thrust of his thinking about them. It culminated in his considerations of the experience of the boundaries of the body and its direct mediation of spatial extension by way of tactile sensory impressions and in his notion of the "periodicalizing rhythm of the somatic feeling of life." Both offer bridges from subjective inner experiences to the "space-time world" - and that neither by the philosophical detour of ontological assumptions nor the eidetic-phenomenological construction of outer reality.

I submit that the suggestion of this 'direct' transition from inner duration to the experience of space and time, mediated by the somatic feeling of life, is the most important of various genuine contributions made by Schutz in the manuscripts of 1924-1928. It was an early attempt at demonstrating the existence of a direct link between human experience and the 'outer world' - offered long before Merleau-Ponty made it into a crucial topic of his investigations - and thus at facing the most elementary yet most vexing problem of the phenomenological approach. Where Husserl's transcendental ego - as Schutz concluded about 35 years later - teetered on the brink of the solipsistic trap, Schutz's Bergson-inspired and Scheler-supported 'naive' phenomenal-psychological considerations led to the elementary access lane of immediate somatic experiences. Insofar as these experiences become conscious, they make external space a certainty for the budding human individual - and that likely before he or she gains a clear grasp of the 'outside' existence of "relevant others," not to mention the grasp of his or her own self.

I am well aware that these rudimentary considerations point to an extensive field of complex investigations to which, since 1925, many contributions have been made. But, to my knowledge, they have as yet not exhausted the task.

CHAPTER 8

REACHING BEYOND BERGSON:

SYNCRETISM, INCONSISTENCIES, AND TRANSCENDENCES

In the last chapter, I have dwelled on a most important contribution to phenomenological psychology made by Schutz in the Bergsonian manuscripts: the treatment of the somatic substratum which has a direct influence on ego's awareness of the 'outside world' of space and time. I attributed to it the same significance in Schutz's life work as that accruing to his emerging ideas about the central place of the ego in the psychology of consciousness. Thus, I will continue my account by taking up the egological theme in the LIFE FORMS. It will be noticed that the present chapter, in contrast to the preceding one, bears not a straight-forward title. That is so because I am not able to offer a straight-forward exposition of its theme.

SYNCRETISM OF METHODS

We are dealing with a crucial effort of Schutz to reach beyond Bergson. It introduced considerable strains within his original theoretical framework, even though he did not develop his egological theme as a second theme. Innocuously, he had placed it into his initial outline, not foreseeing the strains which would appear in his ideal-typical theory of the life forms during the execution of his planned investigations. He had committed himself to making the I the capstone of his theoretical system as a whole, and introduced it as the indispensable principle of its coherence.

Speaking in general terms, the strains alluded to manifested a kind of incompatibility between the methodological principles behind the given theory structure and the substantive purposes it was to serve. Schutz's study of 1924-1928 could be considered a demonstration of what is bound to happen if the results of the investigation of consciousness are subjected to interpretation by an ideal-typical scheme and if, in reverse, the confirmation of the ideal-typical theory is sought in introspective data.

Inadvertently, Schutz accepted this kind of trouble when he decided to rectify the inconsistencies in Weber's sociology of understanding. By and large, Weber had developed his sociological orientations and his methodology from the background of the neoKantian approach of the

Southwestern School (Heinrich Rickert). When he included "the meaning meant by the actor" into his concept of subjective meaning, he went against neoKantian principles [1]. Since, however, he did not work out his sociology of subjective understanding, the inherent contradiction remained hidden. It took Schutz's attempt to carry out the task set by Weber, to bring it to the surface as an entirely unanticipated consequence of his efforts.

We may say that he mistook the signs of hidden incompatibilities for terminological flaws (ambiguities) which he wanted to correct with Bergson's help. And, as indicated earlier, Bergson's rigid antinomic presentation of the chasm between duration and the concepts of language re-enforced his initial expectation: The flowing experiences of consciousness can be successfully interpreted with the help of the extreme form of ideal-typical conceptualization. In fact, by considering Bergson's concept of pure duration an ideal type, he was able to assume that Bergson had already demonstrated the workability of his ingenious but risky methodological innovation.

While I do not think that Bergson's durée pure can be called an ideal type, because it cannot be 'tested' by any kind of evidence, it is an abstract construction fitting the theory of its designer. But, as Schutz saw it, Bergson singled out merely "two planes" of theory: duration and space-time conditioned thinking. Setting up this polarized scheme, he ignored "intermediate stages" while his problem formulation demanded that kind of "pluralism" (1982: 18) which Schutz embodied in his system of the life forms. By the same token, however, Bergson stood clear of the complications which beset Schutz's execution of the "pluralist" project.

Schutz wrote that Bergson's handling of the problem made for "a dissolving of the polarity of the unity of the experiencing I" (1982: 18). This unity is not exactly a developed topic in Bergson's writings; but it became central in Schutz's work. Within the confines of his theory of the life forms, it was to serve as ultimate unifying principle of their system as a whole. It would be an undue simplification to assert that this need was created by Schutz's change from a seemingly dualist to a pluralist scheme, but it was certainly a supporting factor. The difficulties started for Schutz when he wrote that the "unitary I-consciousness ... exists simultaneously in all" life forms (1982: 79). Since he had set up these life forms as "artificial abstractions," this statement cannot be taken at face value. It is no more possible for a person to "live" in a system of ideal types than to live in the architectural plans of a house.

When Schutz slittered into formulations of this kind, he did so because he introduced the "unitary I-consciousness" as a theme that - contrary to his assumption - did not spring from Bergson's theory of consciousness. It was his own theme; with it, he unknowingly changed the perspective of his undertaking. He did not discard any of the features of Bergson's psychology, which he had initially adapted, but he moved them away from the center.

Apparently, Schutz realized the theoretical consequences of this shift only after a longer struggle to deal conceptually with the concrete experiencing and thinking I in the ideal-typical manner of his initial conception of the life forms. In my opinion, his great reluctance to accept the failure of this idea sprang from his ardent conviction that Weber's ideal-typical methodology was the one and only possible methodological means for setting up a theoretical-interpretative framework for empirical findings.

The serious personal convictions, which Schutz formed in reaction to his war experiences, motivated him to opt for Weber's sociology of understanding [2]. Concurrently, his academic training in marginal-utility theory led him to the acceptance of Weber's ideal-typical method as the correct method of all social sciences. It was with him during his Bergson period, it stood out prominently in DER SINNHAFTE AUFBAU, he carried it through all phases of his later work, and its explication became the core content of his methodological articles. In principle, it remained unchanged throughout the long years of his productive scholarly life; I have not come upon any evidence showing that he ever subjected it to serious critical scrutiny [3].

This contrasts sharply with the careful and thorough critical scrutiny to which Schutz subjected Weber's outlines of the sociology of understanding. However, one should realize that this critique served the purpose of bringing the underlying principle into the open and made the approach consistent with it. By contrast. Schutz found the principle of the ideal-typical method clearly presented in Weber's methodological writings. Forthwith, Weber meant to him sociology of understanding plus ideal-typical method. The personal convictions which stood behind his acceptance of the first, sanctioned also the acceptance of the second.

Schutz never saw any reason why he should question the adequacy and sufficiency of the ideal-typical method: for him, it was the social-science method par excellence.

Whether or not this tenet can be upheld, I cannot discuss here. When, as I have maintained, its application in the Bergson manuscripts created formidable contradictions, it was because Schutz introduced it as a method of the construction of theoretical concepts for a psychology of consciousness, an area of inquiry for which it had not been created and in which it had not been tested. In all of the work which Schutz carried out after he had laid his Bergson project aside, he pursued his phenomenal and phenomenological investigations by adequate phenomenal and phenomenological methods. Like sociological investigations, these inquiries yielded "findings" or "results" in need of conceptual representation and interpretation. But there is a crucial difference between sociological and phenomenological data: the first are the yield of detached observations by an outside observer, the second result from inside processes in which the doer and experiencer turns around and becomes a retrospective self-observer. Whatever ideas of the 'construction of concepts" we may accept in either case, it is clear that they cannot be identical. They must needs differ both in the ways in which they are derived and in the manner in which they are "confronted with the evidence."

Something of this sort, I submit, was the outcome of the doubtlessly bitter experiences which forced Schutz to abandon the project of the LIFE FORMS.

Actually, while working on the Bergson project, Schutz made use of two drastically different methods, but was fully aware only of one. The manuscripts of this period show, that he was quite adept in using the other one. He had no trouble following Bergson's introspective path, so-to-speak by imitation. In fact, he made quite remarkable contributions with its help, as pointed out earlier. It seems that this, in itself, came easily to him. What Bergson failed to give him was a clear understanding of the methodological and theoretical implications and consequences of introspective procedures which seemed to issue from an unexplainable personal gift, that of an uncanny intuition turned toward one's own 'inner' experiences.

Schutz, apparently, accepted the introspective insights of Bergson as immediately evident to himself. Thus, he felt no need for making the "intuition" in "intuitive philosophy and method" thematic: Self-evident results tend to make the method, by which they are gained, self-evident in turn. The term, phenomenological method, had not yet become an effective part of his thinking. He should only later realize - under the guidance of Husserl's writings - that this methodological self-evidence - in the context of present concerns - was a mere cover hiding the crucial problems of all phenomenal and phenomenological investigations.

In the immediate flow of his own explorations of the working of consciousness, this was no handicap. He demonstrated this repeatedly, and most strikingly in his insights into the changes of remembered experiences over long periods of time. Thus, his account of how he remembered a traumatic experience - that of being anaesthetized before an operation when he was four or five - at different periods of his later life (1982: 62-64) is most revealing. It stands out for two reasons: It is a convincing corrective to Bergson's theory of memory images, and it is a convincing example of anamnesis, here the re-remembering of long past experiences, or rather, the remembering of earlier remembrances and their transformation over time [4].

Aside from this and other exercises in self-reflection, Schutz went beyond the ideal-typical and quasi-geometrical and algebraic framework of conceptual explanations at other occasions. One point of particular interest, here, is his treatment of the vivid present, the Now of experiencing. In his diagrams, this Now appears as a mathematical point on a continuum standing for external time, a point of zero extension and thus no duration. In his interpretation of experiencing the Now of inner time, however, Schutz spoke of becoming and passing-away (1982: 67-68) with regard to immediate experiences and to memory images. Both expressions indicate something going on, hint at events which unfold in inner time and occur in the form of waxing and waning: not two processes, but one: becoming-and-passing-away. This, in the nutshell, is nothing but the "specious present" of E. R. Clay, which came to fame in James's PSYCHOLOGY (1891 I: 608). Schutz himself was at the time unaware of this conception, which he should later adopt and stress (for instance, CP II: 271).

At this point, I will have to stress that my earlier statement about Schutz admitting only an ideal-typical formation of theory was not to imply that he did not know what he was doing when resorting to introspection.

He was quite aware of the difference between theory construction and introspection. What he was not aware of was that the latter yields results that have theoretical consequences. For him, it was a means of gathering empirical 'materials' for theoretical interpretation on the ideal-typical level.

He knew that he operated on two dissimilar levels. He indicated that much already in the initial outline for treating "Bergson's intuitionist philosophy": To deal with it adequately, one has to reach beyond language, move beyond concepts, and initiate a "thrust toward the Thou" (see Appendix 1). In the text of his study, he spoke of moving into the "pre-scientific sphere," dealing there with "the phenomena of experience, not those of cognition." Therefore, "the method of a science of experience can only consist of acts of self-inspection" (1982: 70).

Now, he had two opposite 'methods' on his hands: the ideal-typical construction of a theoretical framework and the introspective way of gathering 'empirical' evidence for this framework. At the moment he wrote this down, this methodological dualism did not faze him at all: As exponent of a "science of experience, he had "no reason to be afraid of the spectre of the syncretism of methods," that is, of the mixing of different kinds of methods "which is feared in every theoretical and empirical discipline" (1982: 70). In his case, he implied, this syncretism was merely a neat division between theoretical and empirical labor.

This seemed to be a simple and plausible methodological set-up. As indicated before, Bergson had developed his theory of consciousness in a fashion which could be called an invitation to Schutz to establish the syncretic combination which, in fact, he did introduce.

NARROWING THE GAP BETWEEN LANGUAGE AND EXPERIENCE

In a way, Schutz's adaptation of a syncretism of methods was another response to the Bergsonian paradox. Yet, Schutz himself mellowed the harshness of the sharp contrasts, which gave rise to the latter, when he spoke of a "relative approximation of duration." In this context, he pointed to one possibility of narrowing the gap between experience and language. Strictly speaking, Bergson's characterization of language fits only one case perfectly: that of the artificial language of mathematical or other formalized symbol systems. Language in everyday life is language beyond literal or dictionary connotations; it is made to refer to experiences, to convey meanings from one individual to another. The precision of linguistic definitions disappears in personal conversation; the words become fuzzy, obtain subjective fringes which allow a speaker to place the intended meaning on the back of the words used, and a listener to attach a meaning to the words heard, to give them his subjective interpretation.

This may be a far cry from experiences-in-duration, but it is a giant step away from the rigidity of language as depicted by Bergson. Schutz aimed at this when he dealt with the symbol functions of language-in-use and the relations between symbols and the experiences which are symbolized, and with the integration of the symbols themselves into a 'higher' form of experience-in-duration on the one hand, and the reciprocal positing and interpreting meanings in dialogue on the other. Add to this his statement that "for everyone ... each word is colored differently and surrounded by a specific aura of significance and meaning content" (1982: 52-60, 128, 162), and you have a quite impressive modification of Bergson's position. The "aura of significance," of course, does not issue from the linguistic expressions and their combinations in speech or writing. It issues from writers and readers, that is, from what they bring into the solitary situation of writing or reading specific items on the basis of their past experiences. The sedimentations of these experiences come into play while they concentrate on what they intend to write or on the text they read. The effects of the combination of personal and situational factors are greatly enhanced in direct conversations. In every case, word associations, references to past experiences or their sedimentations, feelings, and possibly even snatches of comments are invoked both when I formulate anything in order to communicate it to others or even to myself, and when I try to interpret what I read or hear. When we speak of 'endowing words with meanings,' we refer to these and similar spontaneous co-occurrences when perceiving written or spoken sentences: the meaning, as Schutz expressed it later, 'is' in the fringes. To varying degrees, then, we are indeed "approximating duration" in our "symbol-conditioned existence."

This narrows Bergson's gap between duration and language but, of course, does not make it disappear. The difference remains noticeable; seen from this angle, there is room for Schutz's "syncretism of methods." What made the combination of Bergsonian intuitism and Weberian ideal-typology doubtful, was a syncretism of subject matters. It was introduced when Schutz decided to make the "consciousness of I" into the decisive unifying element of the ideal-typical scheme of the life forms.

Formally, there was nothing which could have prevented the conversion of the "consciousness of the I" into an ideal type and to place it in some appropriate manner into the scheme of the life forms. All what Schutz would have had to do - to single out one point - was to ignore that part of Weber's triple definition of "subjective meaning" as "the meaning meant by the actor" and concentrate on the other two parts, which I may sum up as the meaning ascribed to the actor(s) by the detached observer. Talcott Parsons did so, and the factual core of his differences with Schutz in 1940-1941 was indicated by the latter's reproach: " ... your analyses are not radical enough ... as far as the subjective point of view is concerned" (1978: 104). And radical, for Schutz, was identical with aiming at retrieving "the meaning meant by the actor." Schutz had committed himself to this radicalism more than fifteen years earlier. For this reason, he was prevented from making the "consciousness of I" into an ideal type. The half-hearted attempt at doing so in the LIFE FORMS failed because it amounted to treating parts of the intuitively gained "material" (subject matter) as constitutive elements of ideal-typical theory formation.

The impossibility of this attempt may have remained hidden, had Schutz remained within the confines of Bergson's psychology of consciousness; the latter must be considered non-egological in the sense of Gurwitsch's field-theoretical approach. Yet, it may have been compatible with Schutz's "consciousness of I" had he confined himself to what he called the "me-Here-Now-Thus" (see Appendix 2, "Thou and I"), that is, the I in the specious present.

This I may be presupposed in phenomenal investigations, that is, not made thematic in its own terms. But Schutz was not willing to let it go with that.

RUDIMENTARY EGOLOGY

When Schutz began the Bergson project, he must have had a rudimentary understanding of the distinction between the knower and the known. In the course of its execution, he moved toward its clarification and began to see some of its crucial implications.

Maybe he did not move deliberately in this direction, but 'was moved' by the implications of his introspective insights and his reflections about them. Whether moving or moved, he brought this into the open when he spoke of an I-consciousness whose "most fundamental experience ... reduces itself to the experience of unity" (emphases by HRW). In this context, he spoke of "our inability to gain access to extended spiritual realms through rational thinking as long as we bow to the primacy of conceptual thinking." The "rational world of our categorical-conceptual cognition of experience" is set off from the "non-rationality of our experiences" (1982: 53).

I would not suggest that the term world, mentioned here by Schutz, has the connotation of 'realm of experience,' had he himself not evoked this interpretation when, as cited before, he had defined life form as "a stance toward the world which I-consciousness assumes." Seen from this angle, rational conceptual constructions are no longer antinomically separated from the 'non-rationality' of I-experiences, as Schutz indicated in a longer list of "pairs of opposites," as the "world as form ('representation')" is from the "world as experience" (1982: 53). If both are linked to I-consciousness, they are both experienced, and the "world as form" is as ego-related as the other world. This, again, means that we deal here with the beginning of a displacement of the initial conception of the rigid methodological distinction between a constructed theoretical framework and the ways of gaining the subject matter data to be interpreted by this framework. Instead, we find a tendency toward a conception which, through the particular 'reality' inhering in experiences of and in consciousness, lends this "empirical' sphere a kind of ontological dignity which, in turn, tends to spread into the cognitive-theoretical sphere.

Other telling modifications occurred. I have said earlier that the chain-link principle of the life forms does not explain how the linkage is coming about. But Schutz did not hesitate to provide a satisfactory explanation where the scheme itself had none. He wrote that it is only "thanks to the unity of the I" that "a new, more complex and more differentiated, life form originates" (1982: 54). This is an example of what I did refer to when I spoke about making the I-Now-Thus thematic [5]. If, in Schutz's terms, the life forms originated in the unity of the I, they are created by the living ego whose unity is invoked. Freeing this notion from the for us by now questionable life-form label, we may say: The levels of consciousness, which the inquiring thinker set down in form of theoretical constructs, are not his creations; they are grossly simplified imitations of flowing and fleeting contents of experiences which in any particular Here-Now-Thus are but one unique experience out of the unending potentialities of subjective experiences. Only in retrospection will the I sort out past experiences into kinds of experience, classify them in accordance with the 'primitive' classificatory terms which abound in our everyday language. Doing so, I may naively assume that my descriptions are "true to life"; however, I may also become well aware of the inadequacy of our language to do justice to experiences I wish "to share with others." So, I may tell my wife, "I had a dream" and, while telling it, feel a growing frustration about my inability to convey the incredible manifold streaming of the remembered experience, the feeling for which lingers on in the fringes of my account. Mostly, however, I remain a person reflecting on past experiences, trying to sort them out as if I would sort out the mess of the objects and papers on my desk. For this, of course, I do not create a theoretically systematic scheme. My doing here is ever ad hoc.

A thinker theorizing about consciousness, whether he draws his evidence first-hand from remembrances of his own inner experiences or solicits second-hand retrospective accounts of the experiences of others, does not come face-to-face with experiences of or in consciousness at all. The only experience he 'lives in' is that of the moments of his theoretical considerations; and he remains unaware of them as long as they are going on. In his rational procedures, he deals exclusively with a slew of verbalized remembrances and results of retrospection, in some way or other pre-ordered and pre-interpretated by the persons whose accounts they are. True, he does these persons one better - including himself in his ordinary stance - by making the ad hoc way of classifying experiences into a neatly systematic order. But he can do this only for the price of the tremendous impoverishment of the directly given accounts. Schutz implied this to perfection when he called the categories of his theoretical system of consciousness "ideal types."

Returning to the major focus of this chapter, I will try to shed more light on the "experience of unity" which triggered the start of the basic shift which I have discussed above. It began with Schutz's effort to relate all his life forms to a specific I functioning in accordance with the particular requirements of the life form in question.

With regard to the ego as experiencer, rememberer, symbolizer, actor, consociate, speaker, listener, thinker and interpreter, I have mentioned before that Schutz proceeded with forethought: the unification of such roles and the integration of the theoretically postulated life forms hinges on the recognition of the "unitary I." It remained to work this out and present it in that consistent form which would have resulted had Schutz brought the drafts of his study into a final form. That much he promised and expressed in a longer passage, taken from his discussion of the two ways in which the term, memory, occurs in Bergson's writings and in which it was integrated into his own exposition: There is the creation of memories of 'moments' long passed which, however, can be recalled and 'remembered' in the very Now and Thus:

> The Now and Thus consists not merely of something different from something which was earlier. In it, too, I am conscious of the continuity of my duration. I am aware of the individual experiences which I have experienced. The unity of the I is a quality of every 'Now' and 'Thus.' This unity, however, consists of the awareness of that 'I was' as much as that 'I am.' We believe, then, that we have to justify the unity of memory by resorting to the most primary experience of pure duration, the experience of the unity of the I. What, at first, we encountered as two forms of memory, now represents itself - in view of the unity of the I - as two functions of one and the same phenomenon (1982: 46).

This passage contains the core of Schutz's whole egological approach: The description of phenomena of consciousness - here those connected with remembering - is incomplete and excludes full understanding as long as these phenomena are not viewed as phenomena occurring to, and experienced by, a concrete ego, the "unitary I" which alone unifies what descriptively appears in separation.

Memory, then, turns out to be "the awareness of the on-going I." The "unity of the I," expressing here first of all the simultaneous experiences of the two aspects of memory as one experience, becomes awareness of the "continuity of my duration": the I is not only one in "every Now and Thus"; it is also one in the temporal flow of experiencing. Due to memory, the on-going I has a "consciousness of direction"; it knows that it moves from the past into the future (1982: 46-47).

Drawing these points together, we arrive at an elementary egology. For it, we may maintain Schutz's label, unitary I, giving it a broader connotation. Maybe, originally, Schutz set it up as a concept necessary for securing the inner coherence of the system of the life forms. At this point of Schutz's reasoning, however, it was on the verge of turning into a reference to the actual, living I of each of us - insofar as we are willing to explore consciousness at the source: in ourselves.

INTERSUBJECTIVITY: I AND THOU

In the preceding section, I have concentrated on what, in Schutz's Bergson study, emerges as the most important feature of this work: the transcendence of Bergson's phenomenal framework in the direction of a phenomenological-psychological egology in Husserl's sense. It remains for me to correct the impression that, thereby, I made Schutz into an advocate of the priority to the solitary I. This would be strange in the case of a thinker who became interested in Bergson's theory of consciousness as a means of clarification of the foundations of his sociological orientation. His initial outline offered Weber as the first and Bergson as the second figure of his central attention and he placed the "Thou problem" at the head of a list of "categories" to which he intended to reduce the key concepts of Weber's sociology of understanding (1982: 12). Schutz's goal was intersubjective.

He knew perfectly well that the I would not exist did it not exist in its relationship to other I's or, as he at the time preferred to call it in generalizing fashion: in the relationship between the I and the Thou. Or else, as he expressed in in the introduction to the LIFE FORMS manuscripts: "Recognition of self already presupposes duration and the positing of the Thou." The foremost result Schutz expected from his investigations was a "demonstration of the identity of duration and Thou." Taken together, they are the "exclusive primary facts of consciousness." In this crucial sense, the "Thou problem" became - and remained - the key problem of all of his investigations. He praised Weber because, "without naming it, he moves the Thou problem into the center." By the same token, he reprimanded Bergson because he ignored "the realm ... of the Thou" (1982: 17, 16).

Schutz linked I-consciousness and Thou-awareness in the essay on "Meaning Structures of Language": While acting, the I recognizes objects in the outer world which are "similar to my body and thus awaken special attention." Each of them becomes a Thou, seen "as if it too experiences duration which in course and direction is similar to, nay, simultaneous with mine; as if it possesses a memory which executes similar or maybe the same functions as mine." Thus I conceive of its movements as actions "accompanied by the characteristic phenomena of will and imagination which occur together with my specific bodily movements." But more: I see "this object called 'Thou' as if its and my duration display a kind of parallelity, nay, as if the contents of experience in its duration enter into mine. The Thou stands at the intersection of two durations, two memories, two courses of action: mine, of which I have primary knowledge, and those which I interpret as his experiences." This, again, allows me "to presuppose that the same experience, which I have of the Thou, the Thou has of me. I accept the Thou as understandable by me and as being able to understand me and my life. Thus, I assume that I can posit actions which have a chance not only to be observed but also interpreted by the Thou. And I assume that I am able to comprehend movements of the Thou as his actions which, in turn, I can interpret in the manner in which I interpret my own actions" (1982: 127).

This passage is not only the first explicit and specified formulation of the core content of Schutz's theory of intersubjectivity; it is its full-fledged expression. Most of all, it says everything which Schutz, seventeen years later, brought together in his famous "general thesis of the alter ego" (CP I: 172-175).

The significance of Schutz's first statement on intersubjectivity is heightened by the way in which it was introduced. He arrived at it in the course of a discussion of symbolization. The "Thou" is introduced as a "new symbol relation" in relating experiences to recognition in consciousness. The specific attention which is aroused by the appearance of animated objects "similar to my body" results from their standing out "because they can be compared to the memory images of my own past I. Toward them, I assume the same most specific stance I assume toward my own past I" (1982: 127).

At one point of the preparation of the LIFE FORMS study, Schutz considered a detailed analysis of the positing of the Thou by the I. He wrote a one-page outline under the title, "Thou and I," in which he introduced the term, Thou-posited I (see Appendix 2). Due to its terseness and the absence of illustrations, it is difficult to ascertain the meaning which Schutz intended to connect with this term [6]. Yet, it becomes clear that the term 'Thou-posited I' is multifaced. It can connote 'the I which is posited by the Thou,' 'the (past) I which is posited as a Thou,' 'the Thou which is posited by the I,' and 'the Thou which is posited as an I.' Although Schutz spoke of the "essential characteristic of the Thou-posited I" in the singular, he set down terse comments which make it doubtful that he spoke consistently of one and the same 'Thou-posited I.'

His first statement asserts that the "thou-positing of the I" occurs "only in the past." Somewhat later, the following juxtapositions [7] appear:

I: passed = Thou-posited:	Thou index: course of the past as seen by me
I: Now-Here-Thus	Thou: Now-Here-Thus index in reference to my Now-Here-Thus

The first difference which hits the eye in this scheme, is the introduction of the Thou as "Thou index." The explanatory phrases attached to this term leave no doubt that Schutz used it in order to underline that he spoke of the 'Thou as posited by the I.' Yet, the phrase "course of the past as seen by me" has an autobiographical ring; it is amplified by his characterization of the "I which has passed away" as being Thou-posited. I can see no other plausible interpretation of this than that he meant 'the (past) I which is posited as a Thou.' He, then, aimed at introducing two different Thou's: that of the alter ego and that of the ego I was. Both are posited by the same I; none has the immediacy which inhere in the experiencing I-Now-Here-Thus. Yet, they are different from one another, if for no other reason, so for that of vastly different degrees of knowledge and familiarity: "We encounter in the Thou a center of indeterminateness; we know its past up to the present only intermittently, since we experienced it only in discrete stretches of its duration," and "possibly not even in its 'relevant moments.'"

The fragment on "Thou and I" presents the outlines of an introduction to a broader theory of intersubjectivity as presented by Schutz in the "Meaning Structures of Language." Yet, as they stand, both documents have unwarranted implications concerning the twin questions of the genesis of Thou-consciousness and I-consciousness, respectively.

In the Language manuscript, Schutz proceeded from an assumption not touched upon in the fragment, namely, the thesis of the emergence of the Thou from the recognition of the past I. The questionability of this thesis has been pointed out often enough, not in the least by Schutz himself; he rejected it later as one of the forms of analogy with the help of which Husserl intended to demonstrate the constitution of the Alter Ego from the baseline of his conception of the transcendental Ego (CP III: 71-72, 87). Schutz evoked the impression of an unwarranted genetical position by his arrangement of the ideal-typical structure of his system of life forms: the recognition of the self as past I appears on a lower level than that of the Thou. The conversion of an analytical priority into a cognitive priority, however, was unwarranted. Schutz, in his later studies, leaned toward the opposite thesis.

Nevertheless, the passage is relevant because its underlying assumption, which it shares with part of the statement contained in the fragment: the past I is substantially different from the present I. Schutz, by the way, voiced the same idea once more in the manuscript on the "Meaning Structures of Drama and Opera." In two side remarks, he stated that "the positing of the Thou had been nowhere better achieved than in the dramatic monologue" and added in explanation: "it presupposes the doubling of the I, representing a special case of the Thou problem" (1982: 184, 198): The I addresses itself. But that means: The I-Now-Here-Thus turns to the Me-I-have-become in the course of my past experiences and the I-I-was when I did a certain deed or made a particular decision. Thus, I may take the person-I-was-then to task for the consequences of its acting and decision-making.

This is Schutz's early version of one connotation of James's conception of the I and the Me, established in 1890 but unknown to Schutz at the time; and it was his anticipation of the same notion by Mead, not yet available. To be sure, both thinkers gave other connotations to the Me; I cannot even claim that the one chosen by Schutz was the most important for James and Mead. In his later work, he showed that he also accepted some of the other connotations of the term, Me, [8] but the one he hit upon in 1924-1928 remains of great importance as his recognition of the past I, the Me, as the Other who was me. This formulation, by the way, is also a corrective for the initial error in

Schutz's idea of the "doubling of the I." If the Me is "the Other who I was," I would be unable to know this unless I had already experienced and recognized 'the Other' as for what 'he' is in my sustained encounters with concrete others.

If there remained inclarities which Schutz did not completely remove in his later work, it was because he never came around to treat the question of the psychological genesis of the Thou, I, Me, and I in growing children [9]. Thus, he had to forgo this most crucial evidence and settle his dispute with Husserl's conception of intersubjectivity by relying completely on the thesis that the Other is pregiven to me in my mundane experiences, that it, in the life-world (CP III: 82).

This, needless to say, has no bearing on my conclusion that, in pursuing the implications of Bergson's psychology of consciousness, Schutz was well on his way toward establishing his own theory of intersubjectivity.

CHAPTER 9

TOUCHES OF PHENOMENOLOGY

It would be erroneous to claim that Schutz's tendency toward transcending his Bergsonian base line was a straight-forward move toward Husserl's phenomenology. As mentioned earlier, he began the study of the LIFE FORMS after he had scrutinized Husserl's LOGICAL INVESTIGATIONS of 1900-1901 and the first volume of the IDEAS (1913). But he found that they were of no use for his purposes. As long as he worked on the Bergsonian study, he did not look at these volumes again. Thus, on their account, he had no reason for changing his mind. The allusions to phenomenological thoughts he made were occasional and accidental. When he developed notions which pointed in a phenomenological direction, it was due to his own understanding of his subject matter.

EMERGING PHENOMENOLOGICAL NOTIONS

Schutz acknowledged the existence of the "phenomenological school"; in his outline (see Appendix 1 of this book), he mentioned it as one among several "modern epistemological tendencies" he intended to scrutinize critically. But he was already convinced that Husserl was co-responsible for the failure of recent philosophy, to achieve "anything" for the Geisteswissenschaften. Husserl, he thought, had been involved in "essential ontological analysis," the "establishment of irreconcilability," search for unconditionally valid universal laws "for the forming of categories," and the "establishment of the universal science" (1982: 15). This is a rather severe misreading of the LOGICAL INVESTIGATIONS; I do not see how any of the points made could be applied to the content of the IDEAS.

Yet, in spite of his erroneous misgivings, Schutz recognized at least one of the contributions of Husserl. In the manuscript on the "Meaning Structures of Literary Art Forms," he discussed the various "means of expression which help to divest language as expression (subjective meaning) of its mere 'character of communication.'" It follows that the form of the word remains the same, while it is spoken or heard, but its meaning is "necessarily a different one." Schutz added in parentheses: "Approximately, this corresponds to the deep distinction between word as communication and word as expression, which is postulated by the phenomenological school" (1982: 162).

In addition, there are fugitive references to matters of the phenomenological method, eidetic psychology, or phenomenological epistemology.

Comments which Schutz attached to the presentation of a few illustrative cases, are a good example of such references. These cases bring into focus "the parallelity in the relation between that which constitutes and that which is constituted, between noesis and noema ... " Less clear is a second point. Schutz's concentration on the analysis of symbol relations led him to an extensive preoccupation with the conversion of past experiences into symbols to the exclusion of the question of the reasons why a symbolizing I elects to concentrate on a specific memory image rather than any other. While he did not come upon the crucial idea of the intentionality of consciousness, he was able to write, "by an artificial act, we turn our attention to the passed-away quality experience" (1982: 60). This statement not only contains a hint at phenomenological reduction, at least as far as the assumption of the appropriate stance is concerned; it also points to an external precondition or manifestation of intentionality, the act of 'turning one's attention' toward an object. While it can be said that Schutz encountered the notion of 'attention' by Bergson, he seemed to bring it here to a more Husserlian application.

Maybe the most interesting passages, which seem to have issued from Schutz's first reading of Husserl, fall into the range of a phenomenological epistemology. The first to be mentioned is the notion that somatic feelings of life do not acquire their "privileged position" among quality experiences in memory-endowed duration. Rather, I consider them privileged because bodily movements "had already been executed" and have been part of somatic feelings which "belong to me in absolute evidence." Schutz reiterated: "This privileging occurs exclusively because I experience in immediate evidence this action as belonging to me in another form of consciousness - the sphere of purely somatic feeling of life" (1982: 79). Needless to say that such evidence is not identical with the evident truth of judgments springing from eidetic insights by Husserl (1913: par 5, passim). Yet, Schutz's somatic evidence seems to be a genuine non-eidetic equivalent of Husserl's evidence, not its life-worldly equivalent, but its equivalent in the most elementary sphere of human life.

Closely related to this notion of evidence is Schutz's acceptance of the notion of apriority in a phenomenological sense. Having taken pains to refute the Kantian conception of the transcendental a priori of categorical cognition independent of all experience, Schutz believed "to have avoided the main disadvantages of any Apriori because we accepted the world as experience, not as object of cognition." Yet, he too accepted "phenomena which we have to recognize as given data, as fundamental presuppositions of our 'experiencing,' in short: as Apriori of experience." Moreover, as Schutz's notion of somatic evidence underlines, he held that these his apriorities have been in evidence "long before" the apriorities of cognition; the "long before" indicating both historical and experiential apriorities: "they motivate the latter and make them deducible" - that is, to my understanding, rob them of their apriority. Schutz argued that his investigation, undeniably, "has forced us to accept at least apparently aprioristically givens (Tatbestaende), such as: 'inner duration,' 'memory,' 'somatic feeling of life,' 'consociate' (Thou)" [1]. They are and remain "unexplainable residues" yet "are basically different from the cognitive a priori." The difference is that the "a priori of experience admits merely the incommunicability of everything lying before it, but not its non-immediacy," or, as we may say, its spontaneous evidence (1982: 98). Again, these admitted apriorities of experience are not identical with the apriorities of Husserl's phenomenology. But they are considered existentially givens and have to be accepted in their self-evidence; they are not heuristically assumed ideal types. Therewith, they gained a new potentiality: they could now be developed in the direction of Husserl's eidetic-aprioristic insights.

In fact, Schutz took this step within the framework of his exposition of somatic feeling as bridge to the understanding of outer space. After describing the somatic experience of space, he concluded that, "with the spatiality of one thing, the spatiality of all other things has been discovered and given." If this points to a kind of a priori of space, the implications are tremendous: "with space itself ... a world is constituted which is basically different from non-dimensional inner duration" (1982: 104). This notion, it seems, is related to Husserl's "essential generalities" (1913: par 6 and 7).

To me, the foregoing considerations indicate that, when reaching beyond Bergson, Schutz was reaching in the direction of Husserl, even though he may not have been aware of it.

But he was clearly aware of one of Husserl's most famed early students, Max Scheler. He was impressed by him because part of his work was done along sociological lines. Schutz mentioned in particular that Scheler had paid attention to "the understanding of others and the evidence for the existence of the Thou," considering the combination of both the "main problem of the Geisteswissenschaften." Likewise, he credited Scheler with posing the "problem of founding" and linked it to the task of establishing the baseline of his planned investigations (1982: 16, 18).

TOWARD THE LIFE-WORLD

When, in DER SINNHAFTE AUFBAU, Schutz accepted Husserl's phenomenological psychology as baseline for his redevelopment of the sociology of understanding, he conspicuously took over Husserl's "general thesis" of the natural stance (1913, par 27-29) as the originary ground of all dealings with the world of all human experiences, including its more sophisticated cognitive and theoretical interpretations. In accordance with his sociological objectives, he stressed that this immediate world of human experiences is from the outset a world of social surroundings (1932: 106, 190).

These orientations, too, are foreshadowed in the Bergsonian manuscripts. They contain tendencies toward conceptions which he gave their basic formulation in DER SINNHAFTE AUFBAU, and which he later should further develop, eventually combining them under the title Life-World - a title he took from Husserl's work of the late period. [2]

A quite open announcement of the search for an anchorage of the sociology of understanding in the spheres of everyday experiences occurs already in one of the introductory sections for the LIFE FORMS. Here, Schutz explained that he found by Bergson, Scheler, and Weber a number of agreements applicable to the problems of the social sciences. Among them, he pointed out, was an occupation "with what is offered by everyday life," resulting in "the so-called pre-scientific materials" scorned by exponents of natural-science approaches to social matters yet needed for dealing with "life as a totality" (1982: 16).

In the first part of his study, Schutz reiterated these views as his own. On the risk of being repetitious, I will refer here once more to Schutz's considerations which I had cited earlier in different context. He had made clear that he "deliberately decided to work with 'pre-scientific materials.'" On the other hand, he stressed that his "investigation is forced to deal mainly with 'pre-scientific materials' " - and that because there was no other way to get at the subject matter of the sociology of understanding. This subject matter is no other than the "Thou problem." In consequence, derivative problems such as that of symbolization, have also to be pursued on the pre-scientific level. In fact, it was the main trouble of existing investigations of symbol systems, that they treated the topic of symbols "according to rigid logistic principles," thereby failing to study the "origin of these phenomena"; Schutz's objective was "to recognize the symbol problem as such where it originally occurs," that is, in a pre-scientific sphere. The difference of this sphere from that of science is that its "objects are the phenomena of experience, not those of cognition." Therefore, Schutz concluded that the only appropriate method to be used in the study of the phenomena of experience is that of self-inspection (1982: 69-70).

It was only because "a book must needs use language," that Schutz felt compelled "to resort to conceptual formulations," that is, his ideal types. He realized that this created a conflict between his pre-scientific materials and his post-experiential concepts. Ideal types are useful "exclusively for cognition but not for experience"; this is their serious limitation. The latter is further enlarged by the non-rationality of all experience (1982: 70).

In one of the fragments attached to the introductory materials for the Bergsonian studies, Schutz dwelled on the contrast between the reflections about life - as embodied in his analyses of symbolic reference systems - and "Life itself." The latter does not need analytical reference systems; all its states of consciousness are contained in the given Now and Thus; it does not know of a difference between experience and symbol because the symbol, too, becomes experience and thus co-constitutes the Now and Thus (see Appendix 2).

By the same token, Life itself does not need the discovery of inner duration by introspective regression; it is spontaneous experiencing of every Now and Thus of ongoing human existence.

In these considerations Schutz viewed Life as immediate flow of experience, taking it from the inside. However, this same life underlies ego's external experiences, including conscious dealings with his concrete environment, his life situations. In the manuscript on the "Meaning Structures of Literary Art Forms," Schutz referred to this outer sphere as that of "our external real life" and as "our daily life in the outer world." This life involves the individual in awareness of what is going on, in interpretations of what is experienced in deliberate action. All this could not be achieved without "a highly complex symbol system which transforms the material of our inner world," as Schutz wrote, translating immediate experiences into a common-sense "reference system," as I will add. This symbol system of daily life, Schutz underlined, is more familiar to us than any other "because we act in it, live in it with our consociates, speak and think in it." Thus, "it appears to be privileged" (1982: 171-172). Although not further explained, the latter remark seems to indicate that Schutz saw the "symbol series" and "symbol systems" of daily life as the prototype of all symbol systems which are constructed in the non-pragmatic spheres of social life, ranging from religion to science.

This interpretation is reinforced by an earlier remark, which indicates the possibility that "conversation in daily life" presents the "basic type" of communication in all forms. Schutz stressed that such communication is "essentially social oriented"; the person taking the initiative in communication expects "to induce the person addressed to take some kind of position, to resort to a conduct which is oriented on his communication and is therefore social" (1982: 167).

Since the manuscript, in which these passages appear, was dealing with literary art forms, it is not surprising that Schutz set them down as mere points of comparison during his treatment of the issues of the expression, presentation, and reception of literary works of art. The symbol series of daily life serve the purpose of clarifying role and intention of literary realism which "is aiming at the approximation of the artistic symbol series to that of daily life." Similarly, the remarks on ordinary communication were made in order to demonstrate the socially non-communicative characteristics of literary narration, in the prose-tale or the novel. Being accidental to his present topics, Schutz saw no need to develop them in their own terms. Thus, in the manuscript on literary art forms, the symbol systems of daily life and communication in daily life did not become thematic. Yet, there is no reason to assume that Schutz would not have made them thematic in the "second main part" of his planned study, had he had the chance to execute it in full.

While it remains hazardous to draw far-reaching conclusions from rudimentary statements, I do not hesitate to suggest that the quoted passages can and should be read as anticipations of, or at least as hints at, two interrelated conceptions which became the central themes of Schutz's later sociology. The first is that of the life world itself; the second is the corollary of the "paramount reality" of the same life world among all possible "provinces of meaning" (CP I: 222-226, 227-228).

As mentioned earlier in this chapter, Schutz shifted the notion of apriority from the Kantian realm of categories to the realm of experience. His apriorities were the fundamental givens of inner experiences yet also contained the experience of the "consociate," the fellowman whose existence is experienced in the spheres of interactive encounters, first of all in everyday-life situations but also in any other kind of involvement.

This insistence on the immediate experiential givenness of the Thou foreshadowed one of the strongest life-long convictions of Schutz. Eventually, it served him as a final response to Husserl's failure to demonstrate the tenability of his thesis of transcendental intersubjectivity: " ... intersubjectivity is not a problem of constitution which can be solved within the transcendental sphere, but is rather a datum (Gegebenheit) of the life world" (CP III: 82).

In the manuscript on the "Meaning Structures of Language," Schutz added some substance to the principle. Thus, he explained that the experience of objects and their constitution in consciousness occurs itself in the concrete intersubjective sphere of human encounters: the "possible experience of the Thou" is turned into its "actual experience." The experience of the world of objects is a common experience. But what "about the identity of this experience" as made by me and by another person? This question, for present purposes, gains importance not for the answer, which Schutz advanced at the time. (As discussed, he sought the answer in his distinction between subjective and objective meaning, which he attached to his explanation of the relationship between speaker and listener.) Rather, it is relevant to present concerns on account of observations Schutz made concerning the circumstances under which two persons meet in a concretely given situation: "The life of the Thou took a completely different course than that of the I." He and me arrive at the situation from different directions and bring with us vastly different past experiences, unique for each person. Thus, the encounter takes place as an intersection of "the course of the life of the Thou and the course of the life of the I" (1982: 142) [3].

It is not difficult to discover in these suggestions the germs of a conception which should become prominent in Schutz's later work: that of the "biographically determined situation" (CP I: 9). It allows to do full justice to the personal uniqueness, the individual subjectivity of each person. Any concrete intersection of the courses of life of two individuals in a situational encounter occurs as one situation experienced differently by each participant. In this sense, each such encounter is unique because it is a unique constellation of two persons at a passing stage of their ongoing lives. This sets limitations to the comprehension of social situations as well as to the intersubjective understanding of individuals in interaction. These limits, I suggest, are immediately experienced within the life world; they are givens as much as the experience of the Thou. It remains remarkable that Schutz should have realized this as early as he did.

SUMMARY REMARK

In conjunction with the second part of Chapter 8, this chapter offered both evidence for and comments on the emergence of conceptions in Schutz's Bergsonian manuscripts which were neither given to him by Bergson nor ascertainably suggested by him. In the process of absorbing Bergson's findings and conclusions, he proved himself able to transcend a number of the latter and to mark the points of departure of the pursuit of additional exploratory courses of thematic investigations.

CHAPTER 10

A PROJECT AGROUND -

A RE-BEGINNING PREPARED

At the beginning of this last chapter, I will try to shed some light on the circumstances under and the reasons for which Schutz abandoned his Bergsonian project after having arduously worked on it for four years. It should be understood that the evidence adduced is indirect but plausible. The better part of the chapter will be taken up by more positive considerations; it will take up and amend selected topics which bolster my contention that Schutz, in the abandoned study, prepared his transition to phenomenology as presented in DER SINNHAFTE AUFBAU about four years later.

HUSSERL'S WAY OUT OF THE BERGSON PARADOX

In a short autobiographical statement, which Schutz taped in preparation of his contribution to the volume, EDMUND HUSSERL 1859-1959, he spoke about his original involvement with Bergson. As stated before, he turned to him after he had concluded that the writings of Husserl, as consulted, were of no use for his purposes. He gave no reasons why he abandoned the Bergsonian project other than reporting that he found a positive access to Husserl in 1928, after reading the just published lectures on internal time-consciousness (1977: 42). However, there is no doubt that he started the restudy of Husserl, together with his friend Felix Kaufmann, after he had laid the project of the LIFE FORMS aside.

I do not know whether Schutz, early in 1928, postponed further work on the manuscripts of the LIFE FORMS or abandoned them for good. However, I am sure that, had he taken them up again, he would have had to largely rewrite and reorganize them, and to amend them not only by providing the missing parts but also by substantial changes in the content of the existing theoretical parts.

The formal revision of the text of the here crucial 168 legal-size pages of the first part of the study would have been a matter of course; they presented a first draft [1]. But they are in a state which, aside from questions of the revision of their content, suggests the desirability if not necessity of rewriting the whole. After my first careful reading of the "first main part" of the LIFE FORMS in 1975, I wrote down [2] the following:

> The manuscript progressed not in a linear but an epicyclical fashion. For long stretches, "first approximations" were followed by tentative summaries, these by still preliminary but more complex expositions and subsequent recapitulations; and a third or even a fourth cycle may have followed at times. New sub-topics were announced at the first proper occasion, more likely than not to be followed by another recapitulation of prior thoughts which, in their turn, led to the treatment of a different sub-topic, introduced as preliminary to the one which was announced first ...
>
> This manner of exposition indicates that Schutz, while writing the manuscript, explored, clarified, and rechecked any and all aspects of his complex subject matter, discovering particular facets and specific sub-problems which he could not foresee at the inception and during the lay-out period of his project. The manuscript is as much exploration-in-action as it is exposition.

I can refrain here from exemplifying this with the help of details which the reader can find in the published text. But I will point out that Schutz stopped the further exploration of the relationship between somatic feelings of life and the acting I: "We shall refrain from carrying out this comparison in greater detail in order to prevent a further swelling of these unavoidably inflated expositions" (1982: 101). He was losing patience with the pace at which the study progressed. A few pages later, he broke it off.

This, I submit, was an extreme reaction upon the realization of the practically inevitable implications of the execution of a scholarly project under the conditions prevailing at its planning stage. One may say that, with its execution, he 'made an experience' which can be expressed in the following fashion: It is not possible to write a conclusive and polished report about an exploration while one is still moving in uncharted waters. The explorer may be sure of his goal and the general direction in which he has to move; he does not know the details of the course he will have to follow and is in the dark about the hazards he may encounter.

The realization of this alone would not have been sufficient reason for a man of Schutz's scholarly tenacity to abandon his project. He could have discarded the notion that he had a first draft on his hands, and treated the parts he had written down as a collection of explorative research notes. All of them would have been set down with the reservation: subject to re-evaluation, revision, or exclusion in the light of the knowledge gained during and crystallized after this phase of exploration.

Schutz did not choose to do so. He showed this when he ceased working on the project altogether in order to restudy Husserl. This drastic decision indicates that he had by now doubted strongly that the Bergsonian foundation was secure enough to carry the full load of his project. And this doubt, I am reasonably sure, issued from the realization of the strains in his theory of the life forms. Whether the realization of these strains, at the time, included the recognition of the untenability of his whole theoretical construction, cannot be ascertained. But it is a fact that the life-form theme did not appear in DER SINNHAFTE AUFBAU, the book he wrote after the intensive study period of Husserl's then recent writings.

In itself, this proves not conclusively that he had discarded the theme permanently: It did not fit in. He could have reserved it for retreatment in the sequel to the AUFBAU, which he announced at the end of the book of 1932; its first of three major topics named was that of the "sociological person," as he called it at the time. However, we look in vain for the life forms in the list of specific themes mentioned under this topic. During the summers of 1936 and 1937, Schutz worked on this volume - which would remain unfinished - under the title, THE PROBLEM OF PERSONALITY IN THE SOCIAL WORLD. Yet the extensive outlines do not provide for the revival of the conception of the life forms even though other basic ingredients of the Bergsonian project reappeared: duration, the unity of the person, the body and the somatic feelings, and others. The life forms had been eliminated from his list of essential topics.

Although I have pointed out that Bergson's conceptions of pure duration and language have greatly encouraged Schutz to develop the theory of the life forms in ideal-typical manner, it would be wrong to say that he abandoned Bergson when he eliminated the life forms from his thinking. It cannot be concluded that Bergson's phenomenal psychology, after leading Schutz into a deadend, was simply replaced by Husserl's psychological phenomenology [3]. When, in DER SINNHAFTE AUFBAU, he devised the base lines for practically all of his future work, he started his expositions - after a longer introductory chapter - with the statement, "We take as starting point of the further investigations the contrast between simply living-along in the stream of experiences and life in the spatial-temporal world of concepts, as established by Bergson" (1932: 43).

In the nutshell, Husserl did not supplant but amend Bergson. However, it must be stressed that at least two of these amendments were crucial: Where Bergson's conception of duration was fundamentally ungraspable, Husserl made inner-time consciousness thematic. Where Bergson had taken the introspective method for granted, Husserl had worked out his "phenomenological method" with great care. The latter, again, offered at least some degree of access to intuited inner time. More than thirty years later, the Polish phenomenologist Roman

Ingarden offered a pertinent confirmation of this view [4].

Speaking at a congress of French philosophers of language, which focused on Bergson, he spoke about "Bergsonian Intuition and the Problem of Phenomenological Constitution." He referred to Bergson's "almost poetic" conception of pure duration which he conveys to his readers, "in simple images and striking comparisons," as "a vivid and immediate impression of the reality of pure duration." This conception stands in contrast to Husserl's "quiet and almost dry analysis ... which tries to decompose a primitive and concrete givenness into various concepts such as 'retention,' 'actual flowing in every new present,' 'protention,' 'change of the Now into a Just-Now and a just now Just-Now'," and so on. These concepts are tied to one another, forming "the wholeness of the unity of the original flux of 'constituting time' and transform themselves" in "extremely complicated ways and contexts of the different elementary states lived, that is, into something which, for Bergson, would be a mere intellectual fiction ... " (1959: 164).

From Husserl's perspective, Ingarden continued, "all descriptions given by Bergson are merely a beginning, maybe essential and genial in its poetic form." But "they could be bypassed ... if one tries to gain exact and adequate results, scientifically valid and sufficient, and finally communicable from one subject to the other." Doubtlessly, Bergson's theory of intelligence and of the intellectual forms related to action "denies these forms their reality" and, at the least, treats them "like an adaptation of spirit to matter in which it is condemned to live." Simultaneously, this conception is "nothing but an attempt at solving the same problems which Husserl calls the problems of transcendental constitution." In either theory, it is a matter "of learning how the original flux of consciousness" passes "into a multiplicity of intentional acts of consciousness" (1959: 164-65).

A second problem is to find the basis "on which rests the validity of those determinations by virtue of which each thing individually possesses its essence." For Bergson, "these determinations are only relative"; "their objectivity lacks a foundation." By contrast, Husserl seeks "to show how the sense of objectivity and of transcendent reality constitutes itself ...." Also, it can "show the final necessity of the existence of the real world." As soon as consciousness is accepted as given, it demonstrates that the latter, "in its purely intentional essence and in its intentionality," the world is more than "a creation of consciousness" (1959: 165).

Schutz did not live to see these statements of Ingarden, whom he had befriended two years earlier. Given his mounting doubts in Husserl's transcendental phenomenology, he may have judged them as too optimistic as statements of fact but pertinent as statements of potentiality: Husserl's phenomenology, at the least, points the way out of the Bergsonian paradox not by conceptual subterfuge but by phenomenal-introspective means. Needless to say, the importance of these amendments put Husserl in the center of Schutz's scholarly stage; Bergson was re-assigned to a significant supporting role.

PHENOMENAL INSIGHTS VERSUS IDEAL-TYPICAL THEORIZATION

Chapter 8 concentrated mainly on three points: Schutz's combination of his method of theory construction and the introspective meaning of gaining "materials" for a psychology of consciousness; his attempt to render the effects of this dualism harmless by calling it a deliberate "syncretism of method"; and the unintended frustration of this attempt by the introduction of egological considerations into the theoretical framework of the life forms. I will return here to this 'problem complex' in order to deal with some of its aspects which I consider of particular interest.

In the nutshell, Schutz's undertaking consisted methodologically in the attempt to combine phenomenological-psychological insights à la Bergson with the ideal-typical method of Weber. Or, to emphasize the purpose of the syncretic attempt: It was made in order to theoretically harness phenomenal intuitions and introspective impressions with rational methodological means.

As stressed before, Bergson's antinomic conception of the relationship between language and inner experience excludes any mediation between the extremes. Taken literally, Bergson himself was trying to do the impossible. Therefore, Schutz concluded that his 'pure duration' was an 'unexecutable hypostasis." He found Bergson inconsistent when he asserted that the continuity, manifoldedness, and non-repeatability of duration was 'testable through intuitive mediation about one's own duration." This cannot be so: "The last stratum into which we can penetrate is already 'memory-endowed' " (1982: 22).

Schutz was correct when he treated Bergson's concept of pure duration as ideal type. It was this at least in the sense of being a 'pure' construct. But it must be stressed that the other pole of Bergson's dichotomy, the language term, as spatial-temporal form, was a construct of similar abstractness. As far as the relationship between the terms of this ideal-typical dichotomy is concerned, Schutz was amply justified when he called the ensuing paradox "merely apparent." At least, the given paradoxy does not issue from the substance, from the data of consciousness; it issues from the method, the categorical-conceptual dichotomization of two constructs from which the substance had been eliminated. When Bergson introduced the term, inner duration, he transformed into a linguistic thing what he had characterized as 'pure' flowing-along. This amounts to the fallacy of hypostatization, in this case the conversion of a mere construct into a seemingly concrete entity.

I do not deny that, given the structure, functioning, and purposes of language, something of that sort must needs happen whenever language is used. However, in all Western languages, there is no grammatical necessity to speak of Thought, Consciousness, Experience - terms denoting quasi-objects whose hypostatization I have underlined by capitalizing their initial letters - when I wish to express the notion that I am thinking of ..., becoming aware of ..., am experiencing what is going on.

Verbs, in general, point not to things but to processes, events, activities and, as such, are more suitable to connote dynamics and happenings than nouns. The use of the verb form of the present participle above (thinking, etc.) was mentioned as one form of expression coming a step closer to the dynamic subject matter of phenomenal considerations of 'consciousness.' - I cannot help thinking that Bergson, when rendering his idea of pure duration in the noun form, followed a deeply engrained habit of thinking of Western philosophers, reaching back to the beginnings of Classical Antiquity. Bergson, it seems, turned into linguistic necessity what he had acquired in his philosophical training [5].

The point I wish to make with these fugitive considerations is not that grammatical means make disappear the difference between experiencing and speaking about experiences; but they help make the Bergsonian paradox disappear by showing that its absoluteness is created by philosophical thought patterns.

Needless to say, enough difficulties remain without artificially and fallaciously created philosophical brick walls. But when we resort to a consistent phenomenological-theoretical representation of the results of introspective-intuitive self-observations, the difficulties become less forbidding. The most obvious of them relates to finding the relatively most adequate language for translating into words what is essential non-verbal experience. Most adequate, here, means words which in their form and combination are likely to evoke similar meanings - that is, appeal in their fringe connotations to feelings, associations, and inner experiences which are similar in both the phenomenological speaker or writer and his listener or reader. This similarity does by no means amount to alikeness. Fringe meanings, like emotional reactions, are subjectively unique, emerging, as they do, out of the course of life and experiences of the individual, which are necessarily unique. There can be no identity of content, intensity, etc. But there can be similarity of kind. The words exchanged are partially the 'vehicles' which - to confine ourselves to one case - carry intended meanings from a speaker to a listener; but most essentially, they are evokers of meanings in the addressed person, fringe meanings with their unique content which nevertheless agree sufficiently with the unique fringe meanings meant by the initiating speaker. In any case, the chance of a reciprocal 'understanding' between speaker and listener, writer and reader, painter and beholder, author and actor, actor and audience, etc., hinges essentially on this.

This chance of genuine intercommunication and genuine reciprocal understanding presupposes the opposite chance of failure of communication and one-sided or mutual misunderstanding. Both, I submit, are givens of human-social existence in the same sense in which Schutz, in general, considered the Thou as given.

Such being-given means being given in the ordinary experiences of everyday life. That is, it 'belongs' to the same sphere from which Schutz extracted his "pre-scientific materials." As pointed out repeatedly, the difficulties which Schutz encountered sprang both from these materials and his untested method of 'getting at' them. In other words, they led to insights of a quite different nature from the conclusions he would draw from the inspection of his sociological data. The question was whether an ideal-typical framework, constructed on Weberian principles, could be made to conform with insights gained introspectively and concerning a subject matter drastically different from that which had been given rise to Weber's method and to which alone it had been applied, and applied with impressive success. Its use within the fields of a psychology of consciousness had never been tried before; it was an experiment.

Schutz, I have to add, did everything which could be done to facilitate the success of this experiment, if it had a chance to succeed. In agreement with Weber, he declared this method a purely heuristic device, thus allowing himself a maximum of elasticity for changing the content of any of the ideal types he chose to integrate into his interpretative scheme of the life forms. He wanted this to be understood, and took pains to explain that he did by no means resort to Kantian categorical reasoning when setting up his theoretical constructs. While he did not hesitate to say that ideal types are "categorically defined," he did not endow them with aprioristic validity.

I would be the last person not to realize that this makes for a tremendous difference. Yet, there is a line of derivation leading from Kant's epistemological theory of aprioristic categories to the methodological categories of Weberian ideal types: the derivation of Weber's methodology from neoKantianism is a well-known historical fact. I have to assume that Schutz's early Kantian background not only prepared him well for the acceptance of the Weberian notion of ideal types but also guided him in his decision to capture and develop Bergson's theory of consciousness within an ideal-typical framework.

I have tried to show earlier that the difficulties with Schutz's scheme of the life forms originated in his initial decision to view each of them not only as an ideal type but also as a concrete state of

I-consciousness different from any other such state. Yet any of these states 'belongs' to one and the same ego, and it is aware of this fact. So, there are many life-form constructs, but only one ego "living in all of them." By the same token, a multiplicity of egos means a multiplicity of persons. Each of them 'has' but one ego - cases of psycho-pathological split-personality excluded - and this ego is a "unitary I." Consequently, Schutz could insist that the over-all coherence of the system of life forms was secured by this same "unitary I."

This accepted, why should Schutz be challenged when he decided, for his theoretical-methodological purpose, to make the "unity of the I" into the (ideal-typical) principle of the over-all coherence of his scheme? He thought this was correct procedure. If it was, the difficulties which I pointed out were nothing but technical difficulties, that is, such of an adequate integration of the principle into the presentation of the scheme. They could be overcome by further cognitive reflection or, if need be, by trial and error. Indeed, Schutz responded to them in this way. As long as he worked on the project of 1924-1928, he persisted in the attempt at countering the strains in his developing theory of the life forms where they occurred: within this theoretical and ideal-typical system. When he gave up the project, he had not - not yet? - succeeded either in establishing the inner coherence of the system or in making the unitary I into an ideal type.

The decision of Schutz to remove the Bergson paradox by resorting to an ideal-typical methodology was intriguing in its simplicity. However, it had to withstand one test: Any ideal-type, as Schutz emphasized, "cannot be allowed to be in contrast with empirical reality" (1982: 70); it must stand up when compared to the empirical data to which it refers [6].

Undeniably, the data to which sociological ideal types refer are drastically different from those to which an ideal type called "the unitary I" would refer. Of course, the heuristic scheme of the life forms gave Schutz an optimal leeway for defining its contents and to modify it. The question was whether this leeway was broad enough for the dual purpose of bringing data resulting from tangible observation under one roof with such which were intuited by introspection.

My prior considerations have shown that I think this possibility does not exist. The frank admission of the "syncretism of methods" did not help Schutz to escape the problems behind Bergson's paradox. They reappeared in different form in different context.

Let us assume that the use of syncretic methods is acceptable under conditions. This will be the case when an investigator deals with two different kinds of subject matter, each demanding its particular ways for gaining data. But Schutz, in the crucial first part of the LIFE FORMS, dealt essentially with one kind of subject matter: phenomena of consciousness. When he thought of linking two methods together, he was concerned with one method for the collection of data and one method for their interpretation, that is, with an observational method and a method of theory construction. This is a technical distinction characteristic of empirical sciences. Every undergraduate major in sociology is, or is supposed to be, familiar with this distinction. Obviously, there is no syncretism involved.

But, as indicated before, Schutz had pertinent reasons for calling his version of the given technical difference syncretic. He combined one method of theory construction derived from Weber's sociology with a method of ascertaining 'factual evidence' which he grasped more intuitively than cognitively-systematically from Bergson's psychology of consciousness. Since he felt that, in themselves, these two methods were incompatible with one another, he marked them syncretic. But since they served different technical purposes, he felt that he had no reason to be afraid of the syncretic combination.

As I have contended, he encountered growing difficulties in the execution of his project, that is, in the process of subjecting Bergsonian data to a theoretically-interpretative system of Weberian ideal types. This was unavoidable, if for no other reason so because the syncretism was not confined to technical procedures serving different purposes. I am sure that Schutz's subject matter made it impossible to contain the syncretism within technical-methodical confines. In fact, Schutz was not unaware of this at the outset of his undertaking. Providing for a critical section on Weber, he mentioned in his outlines for the study the insufficiency of Weber's epistemological basis; it necessitates resorting to "a different philosophical approach which, to a higher degree, does justice of Life" (see Appendix 1 of this book). In his introduction, he announced an attempt to "penetrate through language beneath language: demonstration by way of data of life whose images are vaguely described by language." Further, he found that "it can be easily established that there are ... a series of experiences which, being effable, cannot even reach the threshold of language." They comprise "all phenomena of duration, body consciousness, and Thou." They constitute intermediate stages between "sensuality and cognition" or "duration and reason"; the relationship among them is relatively non-communicable. Thus, they are accepted as "immediate." Yet, this immediate life, "as our life, is even in the lowest life form accessible to us. On the strength of its existence, it re-enters the Now and Thus of evidence" (1982: 17, 22).

This recognition of the phenomenal sphere speaks for itself. What was missing, as said before, was the concomitant recognition of the need for making thematic the 'method' with the help of which 'data of life" could be established. This, I submit, led to the ambiguities which are encountered in the first main part of the LIFE FORMS. The following examples will illustrate them.

The life forms are introduced as ideal-typical "planes of consciousness." Yet, Schutz also referred to them as "a stance toward the world which I-consciousness assumes," that is, not as constructs of the theorist but as modes of viewing, understanding, and acting toward Self and world characteristic of the experiencing subject, the individual I [7]. Similarly, Schutz stressed the "most originary experience of the I," which is the "experience of its unity." Again, this aims at immediate self-experience. Yet, in continuation of these considerations, Schutz reaffirmed his methodological thesis that the life forms "are nothing but ideal types ... " (1982: 21, 52, 53).

My second example concerns the conception of the "somatic feeling of life" which "belongs to me as evidently as heartbeat and breathing." In a lengthy footnote to this passage, Schutz explained that his "kind of investigation has nothing at all to do with empirical psychology." Exponents of the latter may "refute my theory that all that which is somatic becomes evident only as movement, as the functional factor in our feeling of life." They may point to the peristaltic movements of functioning intestines - of which I am unaware - "in order to refute my theory." But this is beside the point. There are various physiological processes occurring in my body of which I am not aware. If I have some knowledge about them, it is because I have been presented with suitably adapted reports of "strictly scientific empirical investigations of biological and physiological nature." Their results were "subsumed under a scientific-conceptual frame of reference" (1982: 78; 113-114, n. 40) which is "completely different" from that of Schutz.

At face value, this statement is self-evident, and may be read as saying: The frame of reference of physiologists contains nothing which could be used as measuring stick for the adequacy of my frame of reference. However, Schutz's argumentation points to two implications of considerable significance. The first is that the two kinds of conceptualizations cannot be compared with one another since they are directed upon two kinds of subject matter - purely physiological processes versus consciousness - which, by reciprocal conceptual-theoretical fiat, have nothing in common. Therefore, the second is, that the empirical procedures, by which the exponents of the two fields try 'to get at' the facts which they pursue, are radically different from one another. Nobody can discover consciousness in "inner duration" under the microscope, and nobody can discover physiological processes by introspection or philosophical meditation. Thus, fully developed, Schutz's position meant that radically different subject matters dictate radically different 'methods' and that, therefore, the theories in question are as different from one another as the problems of inquiry which initiated each undertaking.

The third example, finally, may be the most telling one. It concerns the "symbol series" which are not merely established as ideal-typical constructs but which are also experienced by the unitary I. That is, symbols are not only concepts abstracted and generalized by the philosopher or sociologist for his theoretical purposes, they are also phenomena in the consciousness of individuals in everyday life and in other non-scientific, non-philosophical spheres of social experiences of human life.

Toward the end of the unfinished manuscript on the "Meaning Structures of Literary Art Forms," Schutz offered his own interpretation of the notion of literary laws of meaning, standard items in German literary criticism. It had been often assumed that such meaning laws express the essence of the Word and are anchored in the "objective reality of language." But there is no universal meaning attached to words; the meanings change whether words occur as objects of grammar, in everyday conversation, or in literary creations. Within the spheres of the latter, words are (poetic) expression, (literary-narrative) communication, and (dramatic) representation. Accordingly, in each of these basic literary forms, the 'law of the unity of meaning,' for instance, assumes a particular form since it serves a function different from that of the other forms. Yet, in every case it can "assert nothing else than the adequacy of the word to the originary experience" in inner duration: The poetic feelings, the empathetic involvement in the narrated tale, the vicarious inner participation in the drama. The "differentiation of the meaning structures" of the three literary art forms issues "from the capacity of objective linguistic materials as such to be adequate to experience." This, and nothing else, is what the "meaning law of unity" asserts as common foundation of the specific literary laws of meaning for any of the three literary art forms. The selection of any specific form for the artistic treatment of any theme is governed by its "specific affectual tones which push toward one of the given means of literary creation. If one intends to achieve the adequacy of the word in objective linguistic reality to the affectually colored originary experience, the word will have to be formed as expression, communication, or representation" in lyrical poem, epic, or drama (1982: 175-176).

The first comment to be made here concerns the way in which Schutz pierced the conceptual shell of Bergson's thesis of the rigid objective space-time structure of language and thus of the word. He argued, in substance although not in so many words, nothing else than James's contention that the meaning is located in the fringes of the words in use. The literarily differentiated "functions" are subjective; they describe the use of language in order to 'carry' intended affectual meanings from the artist to his audience.

Schutz took pains to avoid two misinterpretations of his theory of literary art forms: (a) His "general literary law of meaning" was not meant to be a "general law of language"; granting the possibility of "an analogous law of meaning in other than the literary symbol forms," he merely mentioned that he was not concerned with them in the present context. (b) He denied that his "literary meaning law of unity ... amounts to no more than a tautology." The assumed paradox, "that one makes into a characteristic of the objective meaning context in poetry what is 'poetic' from the outset," does not exist (1982: 176). In justification of this assertion, he wrote the following crucial passage.

> The experiencing I lives in all systems and thus also in that of the symbol series and no less in the system of facts which are to be symbolized. For it, such a paradox cannot appear. However, the latter must occur in the ideal-typical abstractions of independent symbol series if one does not assume that the symbol function is exhausted in the act of transforming that which is symbolized into the symbol. The symbol, too, enters as experience into the stream of consciousness in no other way than the originary experiences which are the ground for the event of symbolization.
>
> A basic experience, which enters into the symbol forms of language and further into those of literature, does thereby not dissolve itself into symbols. It remains effective and mixes itself with newly added experiences of formed symbols; it becomes a new and third experience. The experience, which is literarily transformed, does not enter memory loosely and unconnected with the literary symbol series. It mixes itself with it ... the tautology is fictitious. At first, the law of unity is the law of the literary transformation of the basic experience into the symbol form of the poem. Since the poem, in turn, becomes experience, this law becomes later a law of the originary literary experiences as such (1982: 176).

These two paragraphs, again, show Schutz turning away from the ideal-typical structure of his theory of symbolic forms as that of a theorizing sociologist; instead, he is turning toward the experience of symbols, created and presented with the help of a subjectivized language by persons in non-scientific situations. The encounter with language, for individuals in the natural attitude, whether for the prosaic purposes of everyday pursuits or the vicarious involvement in emotional experiences with the means of the literary arts, is experience as genuine as any other.

Here, we have once more strong references to the originary grounds of all experiences, which give rise to symbolizations and to their acceptance in a phenomenal-psychological manner. And again, this is set down by Schutz as part of the immediately givens of human consciousness. It is not merely irreducible, which cannot be contested; it is set down without any indication as to how the insight into the givens is obtained. And this must be challenged.

As admirable as Schutz's considerations of the originary grounds and the phenomenal characteristics of literary symbolization are, he did not carry them far enough. On the one hand, it would have been most desirable to develop the comparatively analogous "law of meaning in other than the literary symbol forms," and notably in the spheres of communication in everyday life. Maybe, it was the abandoning of the Bergsonian project which prevented Schutz from pursuing his investigations into these other spheres and most of all that of the life-world. On the other hand, the second shortcoming - the failure to make thematic the phenomenal-psychological method which offers access to the insights into symbol experiences - was likely not remediable within the framework of the studies of 1924-1928. In any case, its necessity did not come to Schutz's attention as long as he operated within the boundaries of the project of 1924-1928.

PHENOMENAL PSYCHOLOGY PLUS

In the last part of the last chapter of this study I will touch upon a few philosophical points connected with the central issues of Schutz's work during 1924-1928. Their development would warrant thoroughgoing investigations which, at the time this is written down, I am not prepared to make. But even if they had been made, they could not possibly be presented here [8].

I have mentioned in this chapter, that Schutz saw the need for developing Weber's sociology of understanding as an epistemological necessity and announced that, for this purpose, a different philosophical approach was needed.

One may conclude that this approach was that of Bergson's philosophy. However, Schutz had not at all committed himself to this philosophy as a whole; he confined himself to what, at best, may be called his brand of philosophical psychology. That he had more in mind became clear in a short comment to a passage which, by itself, is remarkable for a different reason. Having reaffirmed that one cannot "break through" the "symbol cover" with the means of language, he added: Such a "breakthrough can appear ... in the most primitive, most originary devotion to his most personal, most primitive, most originary life. Now, everyone may check whether it may be just this devotion to his own life which makes evident that memory, inner duration, somatic feeling of life, etc., are merely <u>mediacies</u>

(Mittelbarkeiten) of experience" (1982: 98-99).

What he thereby expressed is the same answer which, unknown to him, James had given in 1890 to the question of the corroboration of his introspective findings: I am "leaving my description to be accepted by those to whose introspection it may commend itself as true" while "confessing my inability to meet the demands of others" (1890 I: 299). Later, phenomenologists told their students the same. Phenomenal and phenomenological evidence, I may reformulate this, exists in the willingness of self-contemplating individuals to accept data derived from such introspection as self-evident.

In the same breath with which Schutz recognized this, he acknowledged that he had reached the ultimate limit of introspective insights: Behind the "mediacies of experience" lies "the mystery, which is solved by every one of our changes of breath but by none of our thoughts." Continuing - and here I come to the point I wanted to make - he admitted that, possibly, this notion "leads really" into metaphysics. He was willing to accept such an "accusation ... provided one means by metaphysics that truly transcendental method which finds the precondition of cognition not in cognition but in experience, as far as the latter is recognizable" (1982: 99).

The transcendental method, hinted at by Schutz, clearly was not that of Kant. He may have seen it behind Bergson's psychology of consciousness; but, however unwittingly, it pointed toward Husserl. I am unable to ascertain whether Schutz had more in mind than this method; I will merely point out that, in his later periods, he spoke repeatedly about the necessity of entering metaphysical realms beyond phenomenology. He thought essentially about an anthropology of Man in the life-world, which, he believed, could not be developed with phenomenological means but was nevertheless needed as justification of the whole attempt at building up phenomenological psychology of men in the natural stance, being interactively and intersubjectively involved with one another in the spheres of their life-worlds.

A FINAL NOTE

The gist of this chapter can be summed up in a few remarks.

When Schutz began his project of 1924-1928, he had a good conception as to what he intended to achieve. Bergson's intuitive psychology was strong enough to set him out in his explorations of inner experiences but also strengthened him in the decision to avail himself of Weber's ideal-typical method for all theoretical-interpretative purposes. He penetrated his subject matter with great insights and came up with lasting contributions of his own. Therewith, he transcended the base line of Bergson's phenomenal psychology and displayed tendencies pointing toward Husserl's phenomenology. This brought serious difficulties into his interpretative theory which, in the end, proved that his expedient of a "syncretism of methods" could not work.

Eventually, Schutz felt compelled to abandon the project and to seek effective help not in order to salvage the unfinished project but to find ways to pursue his original objective with more efficient means. He found them in his intensive studies of Husserl's writings. What he learned from Husserl should amend many things he had absorbed from Bergson's work.

In the narrow sense, his Bergson period had reached its end. He emerged from his two-year studies of Husserl a convinced phenomenologist, although one who never denied Bergson's significance for his further work; this work time and again showed the signs of the lingering influence of the author of the ESSAY ABOUT THE IMMEDIATE DATA OF CONSCIOUSNESS.

CONCLUDING REMARKS

The more than four years which Schutz spent on his Bergson project, ended in what must have been bitter disappointment. Yet, they were not wasted, and this not merely in the sense of having been years of collecting invaluable scholarly experiences. They were years of considerable substantive gains and the substantial preparation of his life work.

Weber had brought him to Bergson; he appealed to the latter in order to solve problems issuing from one aspect of the former's sociological approach. From Bergson, he appealed to Husserl in order to overcome difficulties issuing from the attempt to answer problems of the sociology of understanding with the help of Bergson's psychology of consciousness. It would be false to assume that Schutz saw Husserl in the light of Bergson; but it is certainly correct to state that Bergson co-determined his selection of that aspect of Husserl's philosophy on which he concentrated in DER SINNHAFTE AUFBAU. At the end of his "Introductory Investigations" for the study, he explained: "We practice ... that 'phenomenological psychology' which, according to Husserl, is ultimately a psychology of pure intersubjectivity and as such nothing else than 'constitutive phenomenology of the natural stance' " (1932: 42).

When Schutz decided to abandon the project of 1924-1928, he discarded his own handiwork without rejecting Bergson. On the contrary, the interest in aspects of Bergson's thinking remained with him throughout his scholarly life. It will be fitting to conclude this study with a few remarks on the persistence of Bergsonian notions in Schutz's American writings.

References to Bergson appeared in almost half of the papers Schutz published between 1940 and 1960; likewise and to a similar degree, they can be found in his posthumous publications and in unpublished manuscripts of this period. Most of these references are confirmations of the acceptance of those Bergsonian ideas which Schutz transferred into DER SINNHAFTE AUFBAU; they need not be reiterated here. However, he went beyond this basic stock in the course of a number of elaborations of the "problem of relevance," which he now considered the central issue of his sociology of the life-world. This concern with the theoretical relevance of the practical relevances of life in all its aspects was not exhausted with the establishment of the three types of relevances: topical, interpretative, and motivational. Rather, it led into the larger areas of pragmatic action, the theory of choice, and the exploration of the various "provinces of meaning" which are so many fields and dimensions of human experiences. It was in this expansion of the narrower conception of relevance that Bergson again came conspicuously to the fore [1].

The Bergsonian key to relevance is found in the conception of "attention to life." Schutz welcomed it in 1945 as "the basic regulative principle of our conscious life": it "defines the realm of our world which is relevant to us" and even "determines the span and function of our memory." It appears at its strongest in the attention paid to pragmatic pursuits in daily life but makes itself felt in all other "multiple realities"; it occurs in all of them as a typical "style of cognition" (1945c: 537, 522).

Relevances, needless to say, dominate choices whenever decisions are to be made. Schutz adopted Bergson's theory of choice; it refutes the common theory that acts of choosing take place by selecting one of two or more fixed alternatives. Instead, he viewed so-called alternatives as oscillating tendencies in deliberations the self carries out with himself. There is, as he wrote in 1945, "just an ego which lives and develops by its very hesitations until the free action detaches itself from it like too ripe a fruit" (1951a: 175-177).

Bergson's notion of the "attention to life" and his theory of choice point to phenomenal activities within one specific sphere of life with its characteristic style and its particular "tension of consciousness." For Schutz, they became foundations for the development of a comparative theory of relevances within the manifold realms of the "multiple realities" of his "finite provinces of meaning." For Bergson, as shown in an earlier chapter, these dimensions were restricted to two extreme layers: everyday activities and scientific endeavors. Within this abbreviated scheme, he unraveled the "problem of relevance" in a remarkable fashion. In his CREATIVE EVOLUTION, he dealt with "The two Orders and the Disorder": There is no disorder; there is only an order of things different from that with which we are concerned at the moment. What does not fit present concerns, in a relevant sense, "does not exist" for us. This is so because "reality is ordered exactly to the degree in which it satisfies our thought" (E.T. 1911: 222-223). In other words: what is relevant to us governs our perception of given situations which we, consequently, order according to an appropriate scheme of interpretation. Insofar as we notice elements of the situation which do not fit the scheme, they occur as disturbances, that is, as disorderly.

For Schutz, these ingenious interpretations of Bergson were not so much important for their specific form and content; rather, he used them in his analyses of the relationships between any and all "orders" or, in his own terms, any and all "multiple realities." Thus, he referred to them when developing his notion of "systems of reference of the appresentational relation" within his theory of signs and symbols. By "appresentational relations," Husserl had identified the underlying principle of "coupling" or association: When perceiving an object we see only part of it but spontaneously appresent its unseen backside. Defining apperceiving as experiencing "intuitively something as indicating ... significantly something else," Schutz merged Bergson's theory of the two orders with Husserl's theory of appresentation. He concluded: "what is sign or symbol for one individual ... might be without significance for another." The reversal of the relationship between sign and signatum is possible if alternate frames of reference are introduced. The distinction between natural and arbitrary signs (smoke, traffic sign) issues from the choice of one "particular scheme" as "prototype of the appresentational relationship." Even the assumption that conceptualizations of any kind are already signs or symbols is based on the selection of a "referential scheme," instead the appresentational one, as basic system of reference and thus of relevance (1955b: 149, 145, 150).

These considerations show that Bergson, indeed, remained starting point and inspiration of some of Schutz's most important later contributions. It remains to add that, given Schutz's strong integrative tendencies, it does not surprise that he linked Bergson to other thinkers, so to Leibniz, to Scheler, and to James. By the same token, he recognized his influence on younger men, such as Cassirer, Gurwitsch, Heidegger, Merleau-Ponty, and others. But, most importantly, he brought Bergson in conjunction with Husserl. He found that they touched upon each other at many conceptual points and stressed the common ground they shared in a number of larger topical areas. So, he dwelled on the connections between Bergson's "theory of multiple orders" and "the phenomenon of appresentation studied by Husserl"; on their common emphasis of "the importance of our bodily movements for the constitution of the outer world and its time perspective"; on the resemblance between Bergson's theory of choice and Husserl's analysis of "prepredicative interpretations" with their "problematic possibilities"; and finally, in conjunction with James, on the confluence of their "new concepts of the relationships between meaning structure and inner time" which "have laid the foundations for a constitutive analysis of consciousness (1955b: 184-185, 1945a: 539, 1970: 16-17, 87).

Schutz considered himself a phenomenologist to the end of his life. He was this, although critically and selectively. Problematics, scope and thematics of his life work re-enforced what originally entered into the spheres of his interest in biographically successive stages: the selective mobilization of notions and conceptions from various sources and their integration in the general yet open framework of his approach. What he accepted from Husserl, remained the mainstay of this framework. But the latter could not have been sustained without the supporting guylines secured elsewhere. The thinkers named in the central part of these final remarks, as well as others I could mention, played a contributing role in forming and developing Schutz's work.

Bergson stands out among them because he was the philosopher who got Schutz on his phenomenological-psychological way. In the later stages of his work, Husserl gained prime relevance. But Bergson remained in the second slot, rivalled only by James and Leibniz.

It is this which justifies the attention which I have paid to Schutz's abortive Bergson project. Its relevance for Schutz's life work is not simply that of an 'interesting' episode in his intellectual biography; it is a contribution to it which cannot be removed from his work without damaging it badly.

END NOTES

INTRODUCTION

1. For biographical details, the reader may consult my book, ALFRED SCHUTZ: AN INTELLECTUAL BIOGRAPHY, published by the University of Chicago Press, Fall, 1983.

2. If some readers should consider this a conspicuous emphasis on a biographical approach to matters intellectual, I would have to admit this without apology. I view the biographical approach neither as the only nor the most important but still a legitimate approach to the work of any scholar. I am reinforced in this position by the widespread tendency, prevailing particularly among American thinkers, to read the lifework of a scholar 'flat,' that is, without consideration of time and circumstances of the origin of its specific parts and segments as if they were invariably coherent pieces of a unitary 'system.'

3. These extended drafts have not been published.

4. After the microfilm copies of the manuscripts became available, Ilja Srubar called the attention of German scholars to the same project.

CHAPTER 1

1. For purposes of this study, the designation sociology of understanding will be used throughout. This is an abbreviated label which is widely accepted by sociologists, even though uninitiated readers may find it odd or ambiguous.

2. This is not a designation used by Schutz. It was introduced by me in a belated attempt at countering the expression, "phenomenological sociology" which became popular among American and German social scientists who 'discovered' Schutz during the Sixties.

3. In a letter to Maurice Natanson, his foremost American student, Schutz stated that, in his young years, he had been a "believer in the truth of neoKantian philosophy" (May 25, 1957).

4. See the comments which George Walsh added to his translation of DER SINNHAFTE AUFBAU: THE PHENOMENOLOGY OF THE SOCIAL WORLD, 1967: 251.

5. For this reason, Schutz did not call on Psychology as such, but sought help from philosophical sources.

6. Neither Bergson nor James developed a method on paper which would have been their equivalent of Husserl's eidetic reduction. Yet, in their American period, both Schutz and his friend Gurwitsch were convinced that, for all practical reasons, they proceeded more or less in an eidetic fashion. Evidence of this will be found in the correspondence between the two; its publication is in preparation.

CHAPTER 2

1. HRW: In the English edition of LIFE FORMS, the equivalent terms for the three kinds of movement are: passed-away, ongoing, and intended.

2. Bergson's works are cited here according to the French originals. The ESSAI (1889) is cited according to the 29th edition, Paris: Libraire Felix Alcan, 1930. MATIERE ET MEMOIRE (1896) is cited according to the 24th edition, Paris: Alcan, 1930. The page references refer to these editions. Quotations have been translated into English by the author.

3. HRW: It may not be amiss to point out here that such spatialization and externalization of the I is that of the self-conception of an individual and his conception of other persons in which, for instance, he considers himself and others as role actors in specific types of social situations.

4. One notices the similarity with the later argumentation of Husserl in the CARTESIAN MEDITATIONS (1931).

5. HRW: Srubar has achieved this objective in a fashion which is the more remarkable as he offered his expositions in a highly condensed form. He covered all salient points of what I have called Bergson's phenomenal psychology. If he did not discuss the conception of "pure duration," so for good reasons: It is not a part of this psychology; as the basically Kantian qualification "pure" indicates, it is a perfect abstraction. For one of the purposes I pursued in this book, I had to face up to this conception. Thus, the reader will find a short characterization of it on the last pages of Chapter 5.

CHAPTER 3

1. Wagner reports having found a passage in his material in which Schutz tentatively introduced a further life form, placed below that of the lowest layer of pure duration. Schutz called it the life form of the "originary experience of the I," and apparently introduced it in order to make thematic the level of the most elementary experience of

the unity of the I.

HRW: Ilja Srubar refers here to a statement contained in my essay on "The Bergsonian Period of Alfred Schutz" (1977). My recent careful restudy of Schutz's structure of the life forms has confirmed my earlier remark insofar as he referred clearly to the unity of the I as a life form. In fact, he introduced at least two others under the same label: the somatic feeling of life and the moved I. However, I must stress once more that these references were tentative and did not lead to the kind of systematic representation of place and function of these 'life forms' in the interlinked system of the whole - a representation which he afforded to the original six. Yet, as topics in themselves, the three conceptions turned out to be indispensable not only for his theory of the life forms but also for the incipient tendency in the manuscripts to transcend this theory.

2. HRW: I am giving the texts of these propositions as they appear in the English translation of the Life Forms (1982: 54, 56, 59, 66, 69), except that I did not set them in italics, as they are in the original and the translation.

3. HRW: It may not be amiss to point out here that there is a fundamental difference between Bergson's pheno-psychological notion of duration and the concept of durée pure. The first, used exclusively by Ilja Srubar, is viable as descriptive and interpretative psychological concept. The second is either a construct designating an ultimate theoretical limit (Grenzbegriff) or a metaphysical term. While Schutz called the "lowest life form" indeed that of the "pure duration of the I," the adequacy of the expression may be questioned and its ambiguity is certain. Schutz himself strongly stated that the concept of durée pure is absolutely unreachable by any method of inner observation (see my discussion of this point in Chapter 5). These remarks are not a criticism of Srubar's factual expositions but a call for caution on the part of their readers.

4. HRW: Deviating from the rule agreed on, I have changed here the term "meaningless" in Srubar's text to "meaningfree." The German equivalent, meinungslos is acceptable in this context, but its literal translation makes it the equivalent of "non-sensical" - something definitely not meant here.

5. HRW: I take it that Srubar aims with this term at experiences issuing somatically from the body, in contrast to sensory experiences which issue from external sources.

6. HRW: Srubar used the term "comprehension" in both parts of this sentence. In accordance with Schutz's prevalent American usage, I have changed the term to "understanding" in the latter half of the sentence: Meanings posited by others have to be understood; that these

egos (beings like me) are either taken for granted or else theoretically accepted, is "comprehended."

7. I have replaced Srubar's translations of these passages by the text of the English edition. As announced, I will continue this practice in all further cases.

8. Schutz says here still "supra-Individuality" (Ueberindividualitaet).

9. Thus, he speaks of "concepts of daily life" (1974: 38).

10. Compare Husserl's Logic (1900-1901).

11. HRW: The trouble, not with Srubar's exposition but with Schutz's section on "The Life Form of Conceptual Thinking" (1982: 130-131), is that it addresses its topic only in a few introductory lines and swerves into a critique of the "Platonic-Kantian system" after the surprising statement that it is not necessary to investigate the symbolic relation of this life form to that of speech. In his attempt at filling out this gap, Srubar had to rely on additional scattered passages. The doubt he voiced about the intended scope of the life form of conceptual thinking arises again with the cited sentence: it is not at all clear whether Schutz meant it as a correction of the traditional treatment of abstract concepts or as statement of an alternate approach ignoring the whole Platonic-Kantian tradition.

12. HRW: I understand this to mean: to make sense in terms of the theory of the linkage between adjacent life forms.

13. HRW: I am confident that Ilja Srubar shares my conviction that the relationship between mathematical or logical abstractions, scientific or philosophical concepts and the linguistic forms of thinking in everyday life constitutes a quite difficult and complex subject matter warranting thorough investigations aside from Schutz's theory of life forms which he did not carry over into his later work.

14. HRW: Again, I think that Srubar will agree that this statement may be amended by the phrase, 'meaningless in terms of Schutz's approach.' I will add that I suspect some of Schutz's fugitive critical remarks against Platonism, etc., to be implicit anticipations of Husserl's later bitter criticism of Western Science whose proponents have forgotten its roots.

15. See Max Weber, WIRTSCHAFT UND GESELLSCHAFT I, 5th ed. Tuebingen: 1972: p. 1.

16. R. Grathoff calls attention to the predicative character of the concept of meaning in Schutz's published work. Compare G.'s "Ansaetze zu einer Theorie sozialen Handelns by A. Schutz." NEUE

PHILOSOPHISCHE HEFTE 9, 1976.

17. HRW: This presentation concentrates on that aspect of Schutz's theory of the establishment of meaning which reflects his Bergsonian insights. I think that Srubar would agree that this is not the whole picture. Schutz also, and prominently so, spoke of the establishment of the meaning of human conduct after it has run its course. Clearly, the construction of meaning by imagining an intended act as being finished, the plan and the motivations for it are the meaning. Clearly, this represents the model of Weber's ideal-typical case of 'rational action.' In this sense, I may say that, if Bergson was the mother of the thought, Weber was its father. There are other types and cases in which meaning is bestowed by an individual either upon his own conduct retrospectively or upon an other individual's conduct encountered as Thou, and which cannot be called pre-planned ('rational') actions. They refer to because motives, not to the in-order-to motives discussed by Srubar.

18. This passage is explicitly supported by a quotation from Bergson.

19. HRW: I think that the term "paradox" is too strong in the present context. It must be pointed out that we are dealing here with two quite different cases to which the same "philosophical premises" are applied with vastly different results, but not with one case to which two contrasting sets of premises are applied while neither can be refuted.

20) Compare Alfred Schutz and Thomas Luckmann, THE STRUCTURES OF THE LIFE-WORLD I. Evanston, IL. 1973: 35, et seq.

21. HRW: I agree fully with this statement. One may even go one step further and ask: Why maintain the label if it does not fit the context?

CHAPTER 4

1. An astute reader of an earlier draft of this book called my attention to the discrepancy between Schutz's acclaiming Bergson for the "overcoming of dualism of every kind' - as quoted above - and his praising him for forcing modern philosophers "to accept this basic difference between experience in itself and reflecting on experience." However: What, at face value, is a plain contradiction, turns out to be a complex issue of several distinct questions pertaining to different levels of reasoning. (1) The initial "dualism of every kind" is an overstatement; it fits the kind named, that is, the oldest antinomies of Western philosophy. (2) The difference between experience and reflection springs from a phenomenal-psychological necessity. That it is not antinomic has been shown by Schutz who (3) stressed already in the Bergson project that reflection itself is a kind of experience. (4)

Another - genuine - antinomy appears in the first quotation: Bergson's "attempt at constructing ideal types of consciousness." This is a methodological dualism which Schutz had taken over from Weber and which allowed him to adopt Bergsonian conceptions without fear of epistemological complications. In different contexts, I shall return to the last two points later.

2. In the early part of his original German-language essay about "Schutz's Bergson Rezeption," Ilja Srubar posed the question, "Is there, in the work of Schutz, a Husserl stratum and a Bergson stratum?" This question gives me the welcome opportunity to set down my own reflections on the ways in which Schutz accepted and absorbed even extensive parts of the conceptions of others. Proceeding in an isolating analytical fashion, one may construct a Bergson stratum which could be supplemented by a James stratum and possibly others. However, it seems precarious to view the results of such heuristic procedures as adequate epistemological descriptions of the structure of Schutz's body of thoughts. For once, in the third chapter of the present book, Srubar himself has competently demonstrated that Schutz, at the height of his reliance on Bergson, transformed Bergsonian ideas in a quite original manner. The same, I submit, goes for his acceptance of Husserl's phenomenological psychology. Further, even though only scantily indicated in the present chapter, he tended already in segments of his project of 1924-1928, but stronger in his later studies, to bring Bergsonian ideas in conjunction with those of other prominent thinkers -- next to Husserl also James, Leibniz, and so on. To my understanding, the dominant tendency in Schutz's acceptance of thoughts of others is that of selection, partial synthesis, and far-reaching integration. While the origin of a good number of his theoretical concepts and tenets can be credited to specific thinkers - and have so credited by himself - the actual form they acquired in his work was often co-determined by thoughts taken from other sources; in addition, the resulting syntheses were original and received the stamp of Schutz's creative thinking. For instance, his theory of multiple realities, of finite provinces of meaning, is more than an addition of the corresponding conceptions by Bergson and James.

3. This is not to say that he did not find individual conceptions in this book which could be used in corresponding theoretical contexts. Most of all, this goes for passages which could be made relevant for the treatment of the problems of pragmatic orientations in daily life.

4. I do not know why Schutz spoke here of the "recognition of the inorganic." My guess is he wanted to set off natural or man-made material objects from animated objects, notably animals and humans ('the organic'). - I inserted a question mark after the word, practical, in order to indicate that it is my best guess in deciphering an unreadable word.

5. Lest it be concluded that I decided arbitrarily on interpretations of Schutz's points (a) to (1) in the light of my acquaintance with his later writings, I point out that, in most cases, pretty good corroborating evidence can be found in the Bergson manuscripts themselves. Later chapters will bear me out on this.

6. As in the case of other fleeting references to Bergson, Schutz did not give a specific source for this statement. A case for its validity can be made from Bergson's lengthy considerations of "life and consciousness" in his CREATIVE EVOLUTION (E.T.). Here, he presents consciousness as a formative principle of the evolution of life: "It is as if a broad current of consciousness had penetrated matter, loaded ... with an enormous multiplicity of interwoven potentialities"; it appears as "the motive principle of evolution" (1944: 199, 200).

7. Unfortunately, I was unable to locate the preparatory materials for this seminar in Schutz's files. The treatment of Santayana's essay was vouched for by Fred Kersten, who participated in the seminar (letters to HRW: 3/9/76 and 4/10/76). The use of Kallen's study is suggested by the fact that, in January 1958, Schutz wrote to the University of Chicago Press, who had published it in 1914, and urged its re-edition.

8. The alert reader will notice that the expression, "actually constituted," does not refer to the phenomenological constitution of nature in consciousness but aims at the objectively given structure of Nature which is conceived as material reality.

9. I am well aware that Dorion Cairns should be allocated the same importance as Kallen. But, while Kallen had been on the full-time teaching staff of the New School for almost three decades, Cairns joined the faculty as part-time teacher and received a full-time professorship only one year after Schutz's death.

10. Schutz alluded to these facts in the mentioned letter he wrote to the University of Chicago Press (1/17/58). The exposition of Santayana's and Kallen's Bergson critiques follows my original analyses in the extended version of my biography of Schutz (so far unpublished). Some of the formulations set down here present variations of the formulations in the earlier manuscript.

11. That Schutz did not waver in his recognition of Bergson's contributions, can be seen in the summary of his life work, which he designed during the period of his final illness (See 1973: 25, 47, 52-55, 112 for direct references and various other passages for indirect ones).

CHAPTER 5

1. Husserl himself granted Kant a significant historical place in the development of those strands of Modern philosophy which, he found, were leading up to his phenomenology. When he critically dealt with Kant's "transcendental motif," he was primarily concerned with Kant himself (1954: sections 25-27) rather than the neoKantians.

2. This corresponds with the "first cause" of classical philosophy but also with Husserl's originary experiences in consciousness which are directly intuited. In Kant's philosophy, the "main forms of founding" are a priori and establish the primacy of practical reason. It was Schutz's intention to analyze the apriority by Kant, establish the limits of the application of his aprioristic categories and attach to his considerations a discussion of that which is immediate and non-communicable and thus can be referred to only by way of symbols (1982: 19-20).

3. Schutz never found the time to write his own critical appraisal of Kant. But, in his essay on "Max Scheler's Epistemology and Ethic," written in 1957-1958, he dealt extensively with "Scheler's Criticism of Kant's Philosophy" (1966b).

4. This sentence is quoted from the English translation of Bergson's essay collection, THE CREATIVE MIND (New York: Philosophical Library, 1946: 188).

5. The scrutiny of Schutz's first and foremost study on an essentially phenomenological basis, DER SINNHAFTE AUFBAU (1932), brings to light a number of considerations which are fraught with ontological implications. But the ontological problem itself is not posed in this book.

6. The statement about memory was gained by way of a sharp condensation of about five typed pages in the early parts of the original manuscript. The statement about somatic feelings sums up the results of elaborate analyses covering a dozen of pages of the manuscript (1982: 36-39, 76-96); these results influenced the thematic of all later sections of the study.

7. Those familiar with Husserl's philosophy will notice that he used the term Dauer not like Bergson used durée but rather in agreement with its common German connotation of persistence.

PART II

1. I am planning to carry out a study which, among other topics, will be concerned with the inner and outer limitations of Schutz's life work, with existing attempts at going beyond these limitations, and most of all, with transcending his work in vital philosophical, social-scientific, and methodological directions. I do not expect quick results. Nevertheless, I am making this announcement here in order to stress that the problems indicated in the preceding passages are not simply unique to Schutz's Bergson project. Or, to speak more cautiously: they will have to be re-examined in terms of the mentioned limitations of Schutz later work as a whole.

CHAPTER 6

1. Likely, the objection will be raised whether I offer here apologies for insufficiencies instead or outrightly stating that Schutz made mistakes or dealt inadequately with certain questions. If he made errors, and doubtlessly he did, I did not concern myself with them for the sake of pointing a finger at them. That he considered questions inadequately is also correct, at least in the sense that he did not follow them through to the point at which their implications were spelled out. And this has been very much my concern, as this and other chapters of Part II will show. Only, I have dealt with the specific items of this kind, which I selected for critical discussion, not in the negative sense by stressing what Schutz failed to do, but by scrutinizing what he did say in order to find implications and to discern the direction in which he was going, even though he stopped on the wayside. This, again, could be considered a purely speculative matter on my part. It would be, were it not for the fact that the topics in question reappeared a few years later in DER SINNHAFTE AUFBAU and were treated there adequately; that is, they showed where Schutz intended to go in the earlier project. This is sufficient evidence for me. To challenge it would mean to assert that Schutz wrote the AUFBAU from scratch after he obliterated the effects of everything he had done before, so that the occurrence of the same topics and problems in both studies is nothing but pure accident. Frankly, I prefer my interpretation.

2. Bergson's memory images seem to be hypostatizations of intentionally induced experiences. I think that we come closer to indicating what happens when we do not speak of memory but of remembering. Paraphrasing James, we could possibly say, "it remembers," thereby avoiding the dualistic separation of 'somewhere stored away' memory images and the act of remembering.

3. I included a longer discussion of hypostatization and reification in the earlier version of this study, linking it up with various cases of

hypostatizations by Bergson's and some hypostatic formulations by Schutz. I removed the whole as a digression of little significance for my central purpose.

4. Of course, I know that diagrams and quasi-algebraic notations are rather common fare in presentday sociological-theoretical expositions, and possibly also in the writings of philosophers of the analytical school. But since this book was not written mainly as an attempt at convincing these sociologists or philosophers of the virtues of the phenomenological approach, I was skipping a pedagogical device which, I am sure, would not appeal to most of those who are likely to be interested in the heritage of Schutz but have no use for quantitative argumentations in qualitative expositions. - Those who insist on documentary exactness, will find the deleted diagrams, etc., in the German original edition of the study, which was prepared by Ilja Srubar.

5. With trifling exceptions, Schutz did not resort to this method in the project that replaced the LIFE FORMS, that is, in DER SINNHAFTE AUFBAU.

6. Schutz made this statement in the context of his discussion of the difference between the word spoken and the word heard. In the statement above, I have assumed that this distinction can be generalized.

7. Many years later, Schutz's friend Aron Gurwitsch published his book on THE FIELD OF CONSCIOUSNESS (1957), offering a brilliant treatment of the Gestalt principle in phenomenological perspective.

8. For instance, one may ask: Where do the excellent remarks on Poetry and the relationship between words and poem, which Schutz inserted into the manuscript on "Meaning Structures of Literary Art Forms" (1982: 163-164), fit into the structure of the Life Forms?

9. The expressions I used go back to William G. Sumner and his FOLKWAYS, with which Schutz familiarized himself in his early American years, respectively to Max Scheler's sociology of knowledge, which he considered already in the Bergson studies.

10. It should be clear by now that I consider Schutz's language theory in its cwn merits, regardless of whether it was called a life form or not.

11. Obviously, for the sake of brevity, Schutz did confine himself here to stating a principle without discussing the complications it hides. The reference to the listener's "scheme of language ... familiar to him" makes clear that the linguistically "objective Material" in question is that of a vernacular shared by both speaker and listener. This is a

first restriction of the principle. Secondly, the common vernacular contains many words which have a number of connotations, not unlike the vocabulary of an official dictionary. However, it is clear that the "objective material" of dictionary definitions is not identical with the "objective material" of expressions used in the vernacular. Thus, the comprehension of the denotative connotation of the words spoken implies and presupposes decisions, on the part of the listener, as to which of the denotative variations of the words of his vernacular is the correct one in a given case. Often, the concrete situation in which a person is addressed and becomes a listener, provides an unambiguous clue to the right choice. In other cases, the listener may have to ask the speaker to explain which of the "objective" variants he had in mind, before trying "to understand the meaning which the speaker meant." If this becomes necessary, an intermediate stage is inserted between comprehending word connotations and understanding the meanings meant. This is a preliminary step of ascertaining the intentions of the speaker: to find the intended connotation of the "objective words" before translating them into meaning.

12. Two things should be set down in this context. (a) With Schutz's acceptance of the phenomenological approach, the subject-object dichotomy was no longer a philosophical issue for him: The bracketing of ontological claims reduced the problem to that of positing objects as objects of intentionality. (b) With regard to the controversial "objectivity of the social sciences," the matter reduced itself to a basically ethical position: the obligation of the sociologist to assume a "scientific stance" by bracketing his personal bias and, with the help of a canon of scientific procedures, to pursue his observations with a maximum of detachment.

13. When speaking of "Schutz's conception of the life-world," I did not want to contest the fact that the term itself is Husserl's. But I wish to point out that he had developed this theory minus the label beyond everything one may find about it in Husserl's KRISIS. Further, I cannot here discuss his final conclusion in 1957 (CP III: 51-84) that the problem of intersubjectivity not only had not been solved by Husserl but on principle cannot be solved on the level of transcendental phenomenology. Whether or not he was correct in this judgment, I will not discuss here.

14. In his mature years, Schutz used to explain in personal conversations and occasionally also in letters, that he was not sure of his answers but that he was sure of his problems.

CHAPTER 7

1. I investigated this in considerable detail in terms of Schutz's life-form system. But the cogent arguments of a reader of the earlier version of this study convinced me that the publication of my lengthy

analyses, in this perspective, would not serve the purposes of the present study. Since I had carried them out with the intention to show that Schutz's ideal-typical framework could not accommodate the whole range of his phenomenal themes, I found it is easy to concentrate on some of these themes without cumbersome detours. I rewrote the present chapter in this sense.

2. There is evidence that Schutz became aware of the strain in his theory of life forms, of which I spoke here. In direct continuation of the passage just quoted, he offered the idea that "pure duration, as unity of the I, embraces both "Life forms of pure duration and of the memory-endowed I" (1982: 52-53). He added a short explanation which did nothing to dispel my puzzlement about the new idea. However, obviously later, he wrote on the left margin of the whole passage: "Better Language study, 2ff." There, he restored the neat conceptual separation of pure duration from memory-endowed duration (1982: 126). "Pure duration, as unity of the I," was stricken from the text.

3. Later, I will show that this notion has implications for the explanation of the transition from inner somatic feelings to the experience of the space-time world.

4. In a similar sense, I could speak of somatic feelings, issuing from the rhythms of heartbeat and breathing as of incipient 'temporality,' a rudimentary feeling of duration in the rhythm of swelling and ebbing, not unlikely that of the acoustic impressions gained from the ringing of a single bell. I cannot possible pursue these notions here; they will have to be investigated further.

5. I should add here the reservation: under disregard of the notion of the evolution of species -- one of the speculative theories of Bergson which Schutz ignored.

6. Since the manuscript broke off at the end of Schutz's treatment of the topic named, it cannot be said whether he would have connected somatic feelings also with the topics (life forms) he had planned to discuss in the unexecuted part of the first of the Bergson manuscripts.

7. A kind of confirmation of this interpretation can be deduced from the fact that, at one point, Schutz promoted somatic feelings to an additional life form. At the time, this was the greatest recognition of their significance he could make from the perspective of his theoretical framework.

8. Schutz did not spell out these implications. The responsibility for doing so rests with me.

CHAPTER 8

1. The most convincing proof for this incompatibility was provided by Alexander von Schelting, probably the philosophically most sophisticated student of Weber. In his study, MAX WEBER'S WISSENSCHAFTSLEHRE (Tuebingen: Mohr, 1934), he dealt with this break in Weber's reasoning from the angle of his staunch neoKantian position. Where Schutz, almost a decade before him, fastened on the inherent subjectivism of the sociology of understanding as the decisive element in Weber's work, von Schelting rejected it as inconsistent with its body as a whole.

2. See my essay, "Intellectual Life Plan and Fate of a Scholar" (1981).

3. Schutz has shown that the ideal-typical method can be successfully applied to matters sociological in his fascinating studies of the types of "The Stranger" and "The Homecomer" (1944, 1945a. See CP II: 91-105, 106-119).

4. This should not be confused with Husserl's notion of the eidos (image of inner experience) gained by an 'essential' insight by way of eidetic reduction, a notion which is also 'related to types' (Husserl's Ideas I, section 79). I am speaking here not of phenomenological evidence but of empirical data.

5. It should be noticed that I changed here from Schutz's expression "me-Here-Thus" to the more adequate phenomenological formulation, I-Now-Thus.

6. This document is published for the first time in Appendix (2) of the present book. - The difficulty with it is that it was mostly written in telegram style. What, in it, was rendered in sentences, serves the purpose of placing the Thou-posited I into the triple time-context of past, present, future; it does shed little light on the connotations of the key terms themselves.

7. I have dealt with only two out of three categories of comparison offered by Schutz. The third one concerns the "relativity of the surrounding world" and can be disregarded in the context of the present discussion.

8. So, for instance, in the essay on "Symbol, Reality and Society" (1955b: see CP I: 216-217, passim).

9. In his American period, Schutz carried around - in his mind - a whole list of essays he intended eventually to write but never found the time to do so. Prominent among them was one about Mead. I surmise that, in it, he wanted to deal with the genesis of

Other-awareness, We-feeling, Me-recognition, and I-consciousness in the social experiences of young children. His correspondence with other scholars contains evidence that he was quite aware of the importance of this whole problem complex for phenomenology, even though its proponents followed mostly the example of Husserl and dealt with consciousness exclusively on the level of the mature adult and, thus, took its genesis for granted.

CHAPTER 9

1. Possibly, someone may find a contradiction between the asserted "givenness" of the Thou and the elaborate thematization of the "Thou problem" which Schutz announced in the LIFE FORMS and which, in his later work, he repeatedly and prominently treated as the "problem of intersubjectivity." The latter can be discarded: the problem is essentially that of Husserl's transcendental intersubjectivity - a different matter altogether. As to the "givenness" of the Thou in everyday life, respectively the life-world, I will remark: That which is existentially given is thereby not exempt from examination. What, to me in the natural stance, is unquestionably given, calls for scrutiny by me, the reflecting theorist. Or so I have been told by a number of phenomenologists. Without such scrutiny, I could not even state that 'something' is given existentially or, in Kantian terms, aprioristically.

2. See Note 10 to Chapter 5.

3. Schutz spoke of the intersecting of two courses of life "in order to use an image repeatedly invoked." Likely, he referred to Georg Simmel, whose SOCIOLOGY had appeared in 1890 and, in 1923, became available in an enlarged third edition. One of its chapters was called "Die Kreuzung sozialer Kreise" (The Crossing of Social Circles). Actually, it dealt with the question of an individual's membership in diverse social circles or groups, and with the effects of such multiple membership on his personality. Schutz's idea of the intersection of the life paths of individuals constitutes an independent variation and, in one sense, a reversal of Simmel's original conception.

CHAPTER 10

1. The existent pieces of the second part, in form independent of the project outline, were also unfinished. Stylistically, they stand in sharp contrast to the theoretical manuscript of the first part. They are much more coherent in themselves, smooth in style, and almost 'ready for the printer.'

2. I integrated these remarks into Chapter 6 of the unpublished extended draft of my biography of Schutz.

3. My expositions are in no way meant to refute my earlier contention that Bergson remained important for Schutz's later work.

4. I am obliged to Ilja Srubar for calling my attention to this paper by Ingarden. It was presented and published in French. The translations of its title and the quoted passages are my own.

5. I am aware of the fact that the participle form is easily changed into a noun: the thinking, the experiencing, etc. But I am here not concerned with the grammatical trick of the gerund.

6. The question may be asked: Why should all ideal types be tied to empirical matters? I can confine myself to answering that, in the present study, the ideal type appears as it has been defined by Weber and accepted by Schutz. I do not contest the privilege of anyone to call conceptual abstraction without empirical references 'ideal types'; but I consider it my privilege not to follow his or her example, as I do not wish to create terminological confusions in my writings.

7. I remark in passing that the designation of life forms as stances of consciousness introduces an intentional moment into the considerations. It points to a whole new area of investigations which, however, was at the time not opened up by Schutz.

8. Should I be given the time and intellectual strength, I will carry out such an investigation within the framework of the project I mentioned in the introduction to Part II (Note 1).

CONCLUDING REMARKS

1. The expositions that follow are selectively based on two sections of Chapter 16 of the (unpublished) extended version of my biography of Schutz.

APPENDICES

I. OUTLINE FOR LIFE FORMS AND MEANING STRUCTURE

by Alfred Schutz

Introductory Remark by HRW: This comprehensive outline was obtained by telescoping two outline drafts into each other under use of shorter parts of two other fragments. I do not consider it necessary to identify in detail the origin of every section or sub-section of this outline. Occasionally, I had to provide headings for sections or sub-sections or to insert a few words into the outline text in order to secure a minimum of coherence. These additions have been placed in square brackets.

The handwritten source documents for this outline have been taken from the collection 1925-1927a. They comprise:

(a) "Einleitung" and "I. Hauptabschnitt," 1 page

(b) "Einleitung: Leben und Erkennen," Chs. I-III, 4 pages

(c) "Hauptdisposition," page 4 of four-page fragment

(d) "Zur Lehre von den Lebensformen und der Analyse der Symbolbegriffe," page 5 of five-page Fragment

The originals of these documents have been published by Ilja Srubar in the appendix to Schutz, THEORIE DER LEBENSFORMEN (Entwurf A-D, 1981: 319-337).

MAIN OUTLINE

Introduction

(A) Life and Cognition

Sciences of Life and Geisteswissenschaften
Crisis of Epistemology and Logic
[to be] demonstrated on: Theory of Art
Linguistics
Philosophy of History
Philosophy of Nature
Philosophy of Law
Social Economy
Logic itself

(B) [Approaches and Objectives]

(1) Applicability of [the approaches gained from] modern epistemological tendencies to the Social Sciences.

The Neo-Kantians - Phenomenologists - Cassirer - Simmel
Bergson's attempt at a philosophy of Duration
Scheler; Max Weber

(2) Subject matter and method of the investigation

Goal of the Investigation
Its difficulties - Results hoped for -
Proposed method - its justification

Main Outline

[Access to the Central Problem of the Project]

(A) Attempt of Gaining Access by Way of Kant and the Apriori-Theory

(1) Scheler's problem of founding (Fundierungsproblem)

(2) Bergson's attempt at a solution - its significance, its inadequacy

(3) Main forms of the problem of Founding in the philosophy of Kant - "Apriority," "Primacy of Practical Reason" -

Analysis of the Apriori - the given sensory manifoldness - Categories and the limits of their Application - The Immediate and the Non-Communicable - Symbol Systems

(4) Life Forms as intermediate phases between the sensory manifold as 'Given' and as 'Science.'

Communicability and Evidence - Planes of Consciousness and Forms of Life - Modifications of experiences through and in Symbolism - Evidence as Being-Here of the Being thus (Daseiendes als Sosceiendes).

(B) Weber's Attempt of a Sociology of Understanding

(1) Extraction of the Categories:

Reality, Meaning, Understanding, Causal Adequacy, Rational and other Action, Chance, 'to be oriented toward,' Machinery of Power etc., Ideal Type, Type as such.

(2) Reduction of these categories to the Thou-Problem, Reality, Becoming and passing-away (Werden und Entwerden), Symbolic Action.

(3) Weber's social-scientific Categories and Logic:

(a)	Dilthey	How do these authors attempt to solve
(b)	Rickert	the Thou-Problem and the Meaning-Problem?
(c)	Lask	Critique and Demonstration of
(d)	Scheler	Insolvability

(4) Weber's social-scientific Categories in their practical application in the Work of Max Weber himself:

(a)	Economic	Here results beyond all
(b)	Religion-sociological	auxiliary constructions.
(c)	Law-sociological	The break-through to the
(d)	Historical-Philosophical	basic problems of the Geisteswissenshaten.

(5) Result: The epistemological basis does not suffice for the explanation of the basic facts of Sociology. Therefore, the attempt of a different philosophical approach which does justice, to a higher degree, to Life and thus to the basic phenomena of Sociology.

(C) Bergson's Intuitionist Philosophy

(1) Representation of the non-biological part:

Duration, Memory, Reality, Matter and Intellect. Attention Action, Thinking, Social Conditioning. Space/Time, Finalism (Teleology?), Will, Freedom.

(2) The Critique: Missing:

Extensives out of Intensives. Recognition of the Inorganic in Action. (practical line of the intellect), problem of Science and Intuition; "Unity of the Ego" and Social Personality. What is symbol?

(3) Requirements of a Vitalist Philosophy:

Room for Thou and Meaning Problem, Understanding, Type, Symbol, Social Conditioning, Mechanism and Technique of 'Simultaneity' in Space and Time of Life.

(4) Method of such an Investigation:

translinguistic, beyond concepts, thrust toward the Thou.

(D) Attempt of Gaining Access by Way of Bergson and the Philosophy of Duration.

(1) About the Unity of the I in Duration --
Pure Duration, its Nature and its Criteria

(2) Critique of these Criteria yields the recognition that the last accessible sphere is already memory-endowed - Reason for this - Pure Duration as mere Postulate -

(3) Memory transforms experience into symbol - Reasons for this.

(4) Interpretation of the process of grounding in terms of the philosophy of duration.

(5) Life and Thinking; Symbol and Reflection; Meaninglessness of stream of experiencing (Ablauf); Meaning-endowment of what has passed; the Prism.

Main Part I: Theory of Life Forms and Symbol concept [or] Theory of Life Forms and Analysis of Symbol Strata

Introductory: How does one arrive at the type of the Life Form? What is this concept supposed to achieve?

(A) Life Form and symbol Concept

(1) Ideal-typical structure; auxiliary hypothesis; their conditions: dissolution in the general concept of life of the psychological person.

(2) Selection of concrete life forms;
life form and symbol concept.
Selection on the basis of correlativity.

(B) Short Survey of the Life Forms which are most important for our Investigation.

(1) "Reflection"
(2) Pure Duration to Thinking I

The Individual Life Forms: Two Lists

(a)	Duration	Pure Duration
(b)	Memory	Memory-Endowed Duration
(c)	Action	Acting I
(d)	Thou	I in Thou Relation
(e)	Language	Talking I
(f)	Logical-Conceptual Thinking	Thinking I (Interpreting I)

(C) The Individual Life Forms

(a) Pure Duration

(1) Imaginability (Vorstellbarkeit);
Necessity of the Liminal Concept (Grenbegriff)
Consciousness ... [Word undecypherable]
Duration of Things

(2) World view of experiences of quality in the pure Present fiction of consciousness

Excursus on and definition of 'experience'
Lack of intensivity

(3) Impossibility of a symbol relation by lack of an act of consciousness
Why can one not go behind memory?

(4) Pure Duration and immortality
Lethe, theory of amnesia, Jean Paul

(b) Memory-Endowed Duration

(1) Characteristics and functions of memory
When does memory work?
Quality sensation and intensity
Repetition of the 'same'

(2) The symbolic function of memory
Sensory image and meaning image (sinnbild - symbol?);
Their interrelations and reinterpretations
The angle n [Greek letter nu]
Symbols of symbols (Sinnbilder von Sinnbildern)
The origin of the past
The act of attention directed toward the present

(3) World view of memory-endowed duration
Discussion of the functions of "superstructure"
The World of concepts seen from the vantage point of memory-endowed duration
Memory-endowed duration seen from the vantage point of the concept.
Expansion of space; time

(4) Deviation from Bergson, especially with regard to memory and matter

(5) (Transition) The image of the body in this life form

The image of the resting and the moving body
The image of the acting body
The limits of the body

(c) The Acting I

(1) The somatic sensation of life
Knowledge of the moving body

(2) Movement; Bergson; duration; concept, space

(3) Intentional movement
Obstacle; action;
Positing goals; intermediate choice
The becoming of the future
Excursus about the concept of rational action

(4) Symbolic function of the somatic sensation of life
The origin of space
Demonstration: extension as such is constructed
through the extension of the body

(5) Somatic sensation of life and memory
The tying-back of the symbol structure
Duration and space: time

(6) World view of the space-time world
Origin of quantities
New significance of the concept of quality
Object; duration
Concept of Entgegenhandeln [1]

(7) Position in opposition to Bergson:
The acting I constructs space
Falseness of the theory of Vorpunktierung [2]
Movement as unity and dissectionability
Intentional movement and memory

(8) Agreement with Weber's theory of rational action
The obstacle (objective, subjective chance)
Directed and oriented action; The purpose

(9) (Transition): constitution of the object
Why does it have duration? Russel [3]
Preferred objects:
(a) The Body
(b) The Thou

(d) The I in the Thou relation

(1) The external acquaintance with consociates
The parallelism of body movements
Symbolically transforming interpretation of bodily
movements into action

(2) Duration and Thou
The supposition of the phenomena of mental
representation and will

The knowledge of the duration of the Thou is aprioristic

(3) The Problem of agreement (Konkordanz) of (a) objects, (b) actions, (c) the stream of psychic life

(4) The symbolic transformation of apperception into interpretation
The chance of understandability (active and passive)
The splitting of the solitary concept of meaning into objective and subjective meaning
The significance of 'meaning' split in two

(5) Origin of (not solitary) affects through the discrepancy between two durations

(6) 'Social orientation': Explication of the concept. Its limit toward other action

(7) (Reduction) The body of the Thou as object of action
Eros and sexus
The world view of the Thou
Symposion

(8) (Transition): collective consciousness
Establishment of agreement (concordance)
Naming of objects
New constitution of the extensive. 'outside' (Aussen)
Participation of this outside in the duration of I and Thou
Giving of names

(e) The speaking I

(1) Preliminary remark: concerning the gap between the life form of the Thou and language; to be explained in terms of the social nature of the word.

Examples of solitary and diadic experiences not expressible in words yet fully evident: music, Eros

(2) The social nature of the word + its symbol function

The act of name-giving and its reaction upon the concept of matter (what, now, means 'quality'?), of that of action, that of Thou

(3) The main categories of the word: adjective, noun (pronoun), verb in terms of their origins. Position against Bergson.

(4) From the nomen proprium (pronoun) to the collective concept
The solitary experience and the establishment of a plural

(f) The thinking I (interpreting I)

(E) <u>The Concept of Symbol Relation and the Concept of Meaning</u>

(posited and interpreted meaning, irreversibility of duration, Becoming and passed-away)

The concept of symbol relation and the concept of meaning

(1) The function of duration:
Irreversible and manifold;
Extreme [?] interpretation of symbols
Extreme [?] positing of symbols
The becoming of the symbol
The passing-away of that which was symbolized
Tension-relation between symbol and that which is symbolized
Necessity of co-existence

(2) Laws of the Symbol Function

(a) Proposition of identity of symbol and that which is symbolized
(b) Proposition of the actuality of the experience of symbol
(c) Proposition of the permanent relation of the experience of the symbol
(d) Proposition of the interpretation and the positing in the identical life form
(e) Proposition of the symbol-forming acts of consciousness

Each proposition to be discussed in relation to all life forms

(3) Positing of Meaning and Interpretation of Meaning

Coexistence
The character of interpretation
The character of understandability
The concept of reality within the meaning system
Subjective and objective meaning

(4) Meaning as Complex Symbol Structure

The linkage of life forms in the total consciousness of the unitary psychological I
Meaning as combined result of the components of the symbol
Relativity of meaning and of the meaning relations

Main Part II: Theory of the Structure of the Objectivations of Meaning: Meaning Contexts without Visible Thou

(1) Formal laws of the interpretation of meanings:
Reflection about the positing of meaning

(2) Apparent meaning-immanent laws:
Grammatical, esthetic, juridical, theory of harmony, etc.
The refutation of these laws.

(3) Origin and analysis of 'values.'
Origin and analysis of 'collectives'
The achievement and the necessity of this concept

Main Part III: Object and Method of the Social Sciences, especially of the Sociology of Understanding

(1) Theory of the social person; collectives and duration

(2) Meaning interpretation and meaning positing; understanding

(3) Objective chance and adequate causation

(4) Social action and its kinds; in special: rational action

(5) Concerning the understandability of meaning contexts without visible Thou

(6) The intimate person of the individual and of the collective
Limits of understanding, race, nation, and historism,
Sex differentiation

(7) The Historical Individual and the historical event.

ENDNOTES (APPENDIX 1)

1. The term could mean acting against or acting toward someone. The latter seems more likely here. Schutz may have used it parallel to the expression, Entgegenkommen, which means meeting someone halfway.

2. This is Ilja Srubar's rendering of a word which was found undecypherable in the original manuscript. In literal translation, the term means pre-punctuation. In the absence of any explanation, I remain in the dark as to its possible meaning in the present context.

3. I was unable to ascertain the identity of the person meant by this name.

II. THOU AND I

by Alfred Schutz

> Introductory Remark by HRW: This is my translation of one of a few short fragments which were omitted both from the original German edition (1925-1928a(f/1)) of LIFE FORMS AND MEANING STRUCTURE and its English translation. The manuscript was hand-written and covered one page. The original text contains abbreviations of words and phrases which I hope to have decyphered correctly. Words in square brackets have been added by me.

Essential characteristic of the Thou in contrast to the Thou-posited I:

Thou-positing of the I only in past (as prophecy ex eventu potentially possible and interpretable up to the Present (Now-Here-Thus).

In the Thou we encounter the center of indetermination; therefore -- in consequence of having-experienced only discrete stretches of its duration -- we know its past to the present only intermittently and possibly not even in its "relevant moments."

Its future, however, remains completely indetermined, due to lack of knowledge (experiences of its total Present, excluding memory, etc., while I in [my] future am relatively determined by [my] actual Present, respectively my already elapsed past.

Thus:

I: passed = Thou-posited	=	Thou index: course of the past as seen by me
I: Now-Here-Thus		Thou Now-Here-Thus Index in reference to my Now-Here-Thus
I: recognized (experienced) surrounding world in reference to me, index Now-Here-Thus		Thou Now-Here-Thus: experienced surrounding world in reference to me Now-Here-Thus

> HRW: Here follow two statements in the same arrangement. Since they relate to both sides of the juxtapositions, I give them here in succession - the left one first:

Relativity of surrounding world in reference to me [is] strictly reversible, [but] in no way in reference to you!

Umwelt in reference to my Now-Here-Thus = as Thou like me (Now-Here-Thus in reference to me), (according to the Now-Here-Thus of my I) supposedly believed imputed (intended, expected, appertaining to) surroundings (Now-Here-Thus of thou - Now-Here-Thus [posited] by me in reference to me and my surrounding world Now-Here-Thus).

Therefore:

[I] can orient my future conduct on Thou, on the Thou modo futuri (grammatical mode of the future) as I interpret it ex modo praesentis et perfecti (grammatical mode of the achieved present)

[But] I can never [orient] my future conduct on myself [modo futuri]; necessarily, the I modo futuri cannot be recognized-interpreted-experienced other than as I modo praesentis

or

modo perfecti: In principle (but only in principle), I and Thou considerations [are] "relative" to the same degree. Considerations of modo futuri belong only to the Thou, never the I.

Modo praesentis ambiguous (doppeldeutig)?

BIBLIOGRAPHY

(A) ALFRED SCHUTZ

The Manuscripts of the Bergsonian Period[1]		German Manuscript Pages
UM 1924-1925	Soziale Aspekte der Musik als Artform Meaning Structures of Drama and Opera	39
UM 1925	Sinnstrukturen der Sprache Meaning Structures of Language	51
UM 1925-1926	Goethe: Novelle Meaning Structures of Literary Art Forms	42
UM 1925-1927a	Outlines and Introductory Materials	
	(a) Hauptuebersicht - Main Outline	1
	(b) Additional Outline	4
	(c) First Introduction and Outline Sketch	4
	(d) Second Introduction and Outline Sketch	4
	(e/1) Bergson's duration	2
	(e/2) More of the same	1
	(f/1) Thou and I	1
	(f/2) Social and intimate person	1
UM 1925-1927b	Lebensformen und Sinnstruktur Life Forms and Meaning Structure	168

Books by Schutz

1932 Der sinnhafte Aufbau der sozialen Welt: Eine Einleitung in die verstehende Soziologie. Vienna: Springer

1962 Collected Papers I: The Problem of Social Reality (ed: Maurice Natanson). The Hague: Nijhoff

1964 Collected Papers II: Studies in Social Theory (ed: Arvin Brodersen). The Hague: Nijhoff

1966 Collected Papers III: Studies in Phenomenological Philosophy (ed: Ilse Schutz). The Hague: Nijhoff

1967 The Phenomenology of the Social World (ed: George Walsh). Evanston, Il: Northwestern University Press

1970 Reflections on the Problem of Relevance (ed: Richard M. Zaner). New Haven, Ct.: Yale University Press

1973 The Structures of the Life-World (with Thomas Luckmann) Evanston, Il: Northwestern University Press

1978 The Theory of Social Action: The Correspondence of Alfred Schutz and Talcott Parsons (ed: Richard Grathoff). Blumington, Ind.: Indiana University Press

1981 Theorie der Lebensformen (ed: Ilja Srubar). Frankfurt a.M.: Shurkamp

1982 Life Forms and Meaning Structure (ed: Helmut R. Wagner). London: Routledge and Kegan Paul

Articles by Schutz

1942 "Scheler's Theory of Intersubjectivity and the General Thesis of the Alter Ego." Philosophy and Phenomenological Research, 2: 323-347. CP I: 150-179

1945c "On Multiple Realities." Philosophy and Phenomenological Research, 5: 533-576. CPI: 207-259

1951a "Choosing Among Projects of Action." Philosophy and Phenomenological Reserch 12: 76-97. CPI: 67-96

1953a "Discussion: Edmund Hersserl's Ideas, Volume II." Philosophy and Phenomenological Research 13: 506-515. CP III: 40-50

1953c "Common Sense and Scientific Interpretation of Human Action." Philosophy and Phenomenological Research 14: 1-37. CP I: 3-47

1955b "Symbol, Reality and Society." Chapter VII of Lyman Bryson et al, Symbols and Society. Fourteenth Symposium on Science, Philosophy, and Religion. New York: Conference on Science, Philosophy, and Religion. Distributed by Harper and Brothers. pp. 135-203. CP I: 287-356

1957b "Das Problem der transzendentalen Intersubjektivitaet bei Husserl." Philosophische Rundschau 5: 81-107. English translation in CP III: 87-91

1959a "Tiresias, or Our Knowledge of Future Events." Social Research 26: 71-89. CP II: 277-293

1966a "Some Structures of the Life World." CP III: 116-132

1977 "Husserl and His Influence on Me." The Annals of Phenomenological Sociology II: 41-44

Publications by Others

Bergson, Henri

1889 Essai sur les donnés immediates de la conscience. Paris. E.T. Time and Free Will. London: Allen and Unwin 1910

1896 Matière et mémoire. Paris. E.T. Matter and Memory. London: Allen and Unwin 1911

1907 L'évolution créatrice Paris. E.T. Creative Evolution. New York Holt 1911

Fink, Eugen

1933 "Die phaenomenologische Philosophie Edmund Husserls in der gegenwaertigen Kritik." Kant Studien 18: 319-383

1959 "Les concepts opératoires dans la phenoménologie de Husserl." Pp. 214-230 in Cahiers de Royaumont. Philosophie No III: Husserl. Paris: Les Editions de Minuit.

Gurwitsch, Aron

1957 Théorie du champ de la conscience Paris: de Brouwer. E.T. The Field of Consciousness. Pittsburgh: Duquesne University Press 1964.

Husserl, Edmund

1900-1901 Logische Untersuchungen. 2 vols. Halle: Niemeyer

1913 Ideen zu einer reinen Phaenomenologie und phaenomenologischen Forschung. Halle: Niemeyer

1928 Vorlesungen zur Phaenomenologie des inneren Zeitbewusstseins. Halle: Niemeyer

1929a Formale und Transzendentale Logik. Halle: Niemeyer

1929b "Phenomenology." The Encyclopaedia Britannica (London). 14th ed. Vol 17: 699-702

1931 Méditations cartésiennes. Paris: Colin

Ingarden, Roman

1959 "L'intuition Bergsonienne et le problème phénoménologique de la constitution." Pp. 163-166 in Bergson et nous. Actes du Xe Congrès de sociétés de philosophie de la language francaise. Bulletin de la Société Francaise de Philosophie. Paris: Armand Colin.

James, William

1890 Principles of Psychology. 2 vols. New York: Holt

Kallen, Horace M.

1914 William James and Henri Bergson: A Study in Contrasting Theories of Life. Chicago: University of Chicago Press.

Merleau-Ponty, Maurice

1964 The Primacy of Perception. Evanston: Northwestern University Press

Santayana, George

1913 Winds of Doctrine. New York: Scribner's Sons (reprint ed. 1926).

Wagner, Helmut R.

1977 "The Bergsonian Period of Alfred Schutz." Philosophy and Phenomenological Research 38: 187-199.

1978 "Between Ideal Type and Surrender: Field Research as Asymetrical Relation." Human Studies 1: 153-164.

1981 "Intellectual Life Plan and Fate of a Scholar: The Case of Alfred Schutz." Pp. 187-196 in Stephen Stousgaard (ed.), Phenomenology and the Understanding of Human Destiny. Washington: Center for Advanced Research in Phenomenology and University Press of America.

1983 Alfred Schutz: An Intellectual Biography. A volume in the series, The Heritage of Sociology, edited by Morris Janowitz. Chicago, IL: University of Chicago Press

Footnotes

[1] A "Characterization of the Manuscripts" listed above is contained in HRW's introduction to Schutz (1982: 4-5).

[2] The dates of publication of the articles by Schutz are given in accordance with the enumerations adopted in 1970 by the present author for the bibliography of Schutz's "Papers and Essays Written in the United States" (distributed in Xerox copies).

All articles have been quoted from the original publications. For the convenience of the readers, I have added (under the abbreviations CP I-III) the places in Schutz's Collected Papers where the papers have been reprinted.

INDICES

Index of Names

Following editorial practice, I have refrained from listing the appearances of the names of the main figures of this study. For Bergson, I would have had to put down better than half of the page numbers of the text - and for Schutz about two-thirds.

Index of Topics